BEAGLE TALES 5

By

BOB FORD

SUNBURY PRESS

Mechanicsburg, Pennsylvania   USA

Published by Sunbury Press, Inc.
50 West Main Street
Mechanicsburg, Pennsylvania 17055

www.sunburypress.com

For information about special discounts for bulk purchases, please contact Sunbury Press Orders Dept. at (855) 338-8359 or orders@sunburypress.com.

To request one of our authors for speaking engagements or book signings, please contact Sunbury Press Publicity Dept. at publicity@sunburypress.com.

ISBN: 978-1-62006-541-9 (Trade Paperback)
ISBN: 978-1-62006-542-6 (Mobipocket)
ISBN: 978-1-62006-543-3 (ePub)

Library of Congress Control Number: 2015931829

FIRST SUNBURY PRESS EDITION: January 2015

Product of the United States of America
0 1 1 2 3 5 8 13 21 34 55

Set in Bookman Old Style
Designed by Lawrence Knorr
Cover by Lawrence Knorr
Cover Photo by Bob Ford
Edited by Janice Rhayem

Continue the Enlightenment!

FROM
BETTER BEAGLING

After a brief hiatus, Bob Ford returned to **Better Beagling** in 2014 with his monthly column "Running On The LIghter Side." Our loyal readers were thrilled and many have written or called to express their appreciation. With his blend of country boy humor and down-to-earth common sense, Bob Ford provides a light hearted look at the sport of beagling. Our staff eagerly anticipates his submission each month and can be frequently heard chuckling out loud and saying, "You've gotta hear this..." If you love beagles, as pets or as hunting companions, you'll enjoy Bob's anecdotes and escapades with his canine friends. We certainly do.

Tamah DePriest, editor **Better Beagling**,
on the web at betterbeagling.com
e-mail: info@betterbeagling.com
812.889.2400

FROM
THE AMERICAN BEAGLER

We were contacted by the publisher of **Beagle Tales**, by Bob Ford about advertising the book in our magazine, *The American Beagler*. Of course, we were interested in running an ad and also requested a copy of the book. After reading the book we contacted Sunbury Press with a message for Bob Ford to contact us to see about the possibility of having him write a monthly article in *The American Beagler*.

We were thrilled when Bob gave us the opportunity to feature him as a writer. We were excited to get a writer of his caliber for a monthly article. We take copies of *Beagle Tales* and the latest issues of *The American Beagler Magazine* with Bob's articles to the Beagle Hunts. We find people laughing and reading the articles out loud.

We are looking forward to Bob's next book.

The American Beagler Magazine
Mike and Janie Ridenhour
PO Box 957
Belle, MO 65013
573-859-6866
www.theamericanbeagler.com
ridenhour000@centurytel.net

FROM
HOUNDS AND HUNTING

We are very pleased to be able to include Bob's writing in *Hounds and Hunting*. His articles bring a fresh, fun approach to the love of beagling.

Our staff anticipates a chuckle with each article, and he never disappoints.

Hounds and Hunting
Since 1903
The Only Magazine Featuring All Types of Beagle Field Trials
www.houndsandhunting.com

FROM
JODY BLACKWELDER

In a time when most outdoor writers are writing about the latest must have products or about an adventure that most of us can never afford Bob Ford is writing about down home values and truths. Reading his stories takes me back to a more simple time of enjoying family, friends, and of course my four legged hunting partners. Bob Ford keeps the outdoor storytelling tradition alive with few pictures and many words. I would like to think Bob for bringing my website to life. Keep up the good work and may God Bless.

Jody Blackwelder
WWW.blackweldersoutfitterjournal.com

Acknowledgments

This book is dedicated to the hounds, past and present, who have given me so many good hours afield. I would like to thank Better Beagling, The American Beagler, and Hounds and Hunting. These magazines feature my writing. I also offer great appreciation to the Bellwood Beagle Club and West Branch Beagle Club--It is good to have so many wonderful brothers in beagling. As always, my wife is deserving of special credit--she has tolerated more than she anticipated when she married a beagle-running, rabbit-hunting preacher.

Anniversary Gift

"Why are they so persistent?!" my wife, Renee, hollered while being mauled by a small pack of beagles. It was nine o'clock at night, and it was their feeding time. They know when chow gets dispensed. They have perfect internal clocks. Hounds ricocheted off Renee's lap, leaped onto the couch and back to the floor, and then they started to run for the door to the basement. When she did not follow them, they returned to her lap to ricochet and bounce again, thinking maybe her clock was broken, and she forgot about supper. I walked to the basement, and they followed me. I fed them each in their own crate before going back upstairs. The hounds would eat and then sleep—until four o'clock in the morning.

That is when I load the beasts into the truck and take them afield for a little rabbit running while I work on my weekly sermon. I let them into the yard to take care of their morning business, and then I leash them to walk the pack to the truck's dog box. The sight of a leash is enough to send their excitement button into overdrive. They don't go for walks in the park, and they don't walk on lead around the block to defecate in the neighbor's yard. The only time they see leashes is to go to the vet or to chase rabbits.

"Ugh," I heard my wife upstairs as she no doubt put the pillows over her head to block the sounds of excited beagles. Their rabbit pleas are even more pronounced than their pleas for food. The beagles sung to me for a couple hours as they chased several rabbits, and I was home by eight. The tired hounds went to the living room floor and assumed the position of calm beagles, sprawled out on the floor and dreaming of another chase.

"I wish they wouldn't do that barking when you take them in the morning." Renee topped her coffee mug and filled one for me.

"Sorry about that," I apologized.

"But look how cute they are now," she cooed with delight, looking at the mutts as they slumbered on the hardwood floor next to the dog beds, preferring the cooler temperature of the wood. One even went to slumber on the kitchen linoleum.

"It's a vicious circle," I said.

"How so?"

"Well, I run them till they are tired," I explained, "and then they are calm like this. But it takes more and more rabbit chasing to get them tired as they build endurance. We are just getting out of the hot months. Soon they will have a lot more endurance."

"Great," she said, rolling her eyes.

When it was still in the hottest part of summer, and the dogs were not chasing many rabbits, Renee was upset by the rambunctious beagles that were full of energy.

"They keep getting into the cupboards," she complained with her hands on her hips as I came home. "Can't you take them to the woods?"

"The weather is supposed to break later this week," I said.

"Well good, because they are eating everything they can get into." She held the remnants of a shredded bag of chips in her hand. The bag was on top of the counter at one time.

"Yeah, they have too much energy." I shook my head.

"They exerted themselves in the yard." She poked her thumb in that direction. I walked out to see where they had started digging along the fence. "There was a chipmunk that ran over the fence. They were obsessed," my wife yelled out the window. I went to the shed and got a bag of ready mix cement to fill in the hole. I poured it into the would-be-escape tunnel and watered the dry mix with a garden hose before going back into the house. Soon the whole fence will have a moat of cement under it as each of these repairs merge into one mass of concrete. It keeps their nails trimmed when they try to burrow through the cement. Thankfully, the weather has cooled a little bit, and they are getting regular rabbit chases in sufficient amounts to keep them tired and free of nuisance behavior that characterizes their boredom.

Right now we are into September as you read this. It is a busy time of year for me. This is the season when I practice with my recurve bow a little bit so I can hunt deer in October—before rabbit season opens. I try to shoot deer where I rabbit hunt to remove the temptation. When they made crossbows legal for hunting, I decided to start using a recurve for the challenge. While I shoot all year round, I pick up the pace in the weeks before archery season opens. Primarily, my main goal is to make sure that I can still shoot my bow with accuracy out to thirty yards. This is convenient, because I always see deer at forty yards or more. For the most part, I just watch the deer walk around beyond my effective range. Sometimes they come closer, and I fill the freezer.

September is also dove season, and while I am not an avid dove hunter, I do find it to be a good opportunity to go with people who are dove hunting experts. Every year I stumble into a good rabbit-hunting spot this way. My buddies will be shooting doves, and I am busy looking at briars and noticing where the rabbits were eating bark on saplings the previous winter.

"Hey, what gun is that?" my buddy said one day while we were waiting for doves to fly to us.

"Huh?" I said, almost coming out of a sleep as I was staring into a thick spot of multi-floral rose and daydreaming about rabbit chases in a month.

"Is that what you are using for doves?" he looked at me in disbelief. I looked down and saw my double barrel .410 in my hands. I was thinking about rabbit hunting when I left the house, and was hoping that this new dove hunting hot spot would also be good for rabbits, and I must have grabbed my early season rabbit gun by accident.

September is also my anniversary month. One of my wife's favorite things about holidays is that I buy a blank card and write my own words in there. The first time I did this was because I had forgotten to get a card on her birthday the first year we were married. I had her gift but forgot to get the card to go with it. She liked it so much that I now have to write one for every holiday.

I was thinking about this year's anniversary gift, and I had a thought. I was thinking that the beagles bother her at feeding time, and they dig holes in the yard, and they steal food at every opportunity from the kitchen. I'm thinking about buying my wife a stress-free week for our anniversary. My home state of Pennsylvania does not permit rabbit hunting until the end of October. Plenty of states, however, do allow for hunting in the month of September. I could write a nice card and then tell her that I will take the dogs on a road trip and get them out of her hair. I'll then hunt for a week and get an early start to the hunting season. She could have a stress-free week with no morning barking or evening feedings.

Do you think she would enjoy that as a gift? I could enclose a little gift certificate in the romantic card that reads, "I love you! This coupon can be redeemed for one week's vacation from the beagles." Notice how I didn't mention that it was a vacation where she stays home and I go away with the dogs? Naturally, I would not leave until late September, after the anniversary day. I am a Romantic at heart.

I was giving more detailed thought to this gift just the other day while running the beagles at the beagle club. I think I should probably have a backup gift in case she isn't enthused with the coupon in the card. I do want more anniversaries. You think she would like a new tracking collar for the dogs? She does love them and would worry if they were missing.

MODERN DOG CARE

I happened to have one of my young hounds in the
passenger seat of my truck not too long ago. I was on the
way to a meeting that started at ten in the morning. It was
with a bunch of other pastors in a nearby town. To be
honest, that seems pretty late in the morning to have a
meeting, but I think many pastors consider that the start
of their workday. I grew up in a house where the work day
started much earlier, but hey, who am I to judge another
person's work schedule?

Anyway, I put in an hour and a half of sermon
preparation in my office before the meeting. When I said "in
my office," I meant that I was sitting on a tree stump while
my young Duke chased rabbits. I was about three quarters
of the way between my house and the location of the
meeting. I carry a Bible and a notebook in the field, as well
as an expensive pen that the office supply store claims will
write in any temperature because NASA uses it. It does
work in cold weather quite well. My Bible and notebook live
in a zip-top bag in case of rain, snow, or falling in a creek.
The latter mishap is not too uncommon when I am trout
fishing in the spring and normally occurs when someone
can see me. On that morning it was dry, except for a few
snowflakes that were being knocked out of the trees by the
wind, which gusted on occasion, relocating the powdery
snow from the boughs of the hemlocks to the forest floor,
which had just enough snow on it to let a person walk
quietly. Duke had brought the rabbit past me once
already, but I was writing something down and didn't
notice it. The rabbit came by a second time, and I drew a
bead on him. "Click!" my gun misfired. I opened the breach
of the double barrel and noticed that I did not have the
thing loaded. I remedied that problem, engaged the safety,
and leaned the old A. H. Fox against a tree as Duke ran

past, chasing the rabbit I had just "missed." I returned to my sermon.

The rabbit could run quieter than I could walk, and when Duke returned, he ran behind me on the rabbit that I failed to see again. I returned to my notebook and jotted down some more ideas I had for the upcoming Sunday, ideas that came to me while I was not noticing the rabbit. I glanced at my watch and realized I needed to get ready for the meeting. I put my books in their zip-top bags and returned them to the muzzle-loader-type "possible pouch" I store them in while walking. I picked up the gun and got ready to retrieve Duke, who was baying in a gully a few hundred yards to my right. I walked in that direction when the rabbit came slithering through some mountain laurel and paused. "Was the gun loaded?" I wondered as I squeezed the trigger. I put him in the game vest. Duke came by shortly, and I leashed him for the walk back to the truck. I put the game vest in the bed of the truck to cool the bunny.

Anyway, I stopped at the gas station before the meeting and had just returned to my truck with a cup of coffee when I saw a guy crouched over and walking around with a bag on his hand that looked like the sort of thing people wear in cafeterias while serving food. He was walking his dog on the sidewalk and was gathering processed dog food with the glove. As I said earlier, Duke was in the passenger seat and started barking at the canine that was defiling the sidewalk. The man walked over to see my dog. I cracked the window, just a little, to talk to him after he knocked on my door with a glove full of poo.

"Yeah?" I said

"Is that your dog?" he asked.

"Yeah," I said again, wondering who would drive around with somebody else's dog in the front seat when a perfectly good dog box was in the bed of the truck.

"He is a beagle," the guy said. "Mine is a beagle mix."

The dog jumped up on his hind legs and leaned his front paws on the driver-side door's window, fogging it with his breath as he barked at Duke, who was brave from my lap.

"You sure it ain't a Walker coonhound mix?" I said, looking it in the eye as I sipped coffee and put the cup on the dash where Duke couldn't spill it. The coffee steamed the windshield almost as much as Rover fogged the door.

"The guy I bought it from said it was a beagle," he said, shrugging his shoulders. "My name is Dan."

"I'm Bob." I extended my hand, with some unease, as he appeared to be collecting dog crap.

He must have noticed my hesitation, "Don't worry, I always carry the turds in my left hand."

"Good to know," I said. "Are you saving them for something?"

"What?" he asked.

"The doo doo." I looked up at it as he leaned his weight upon his forearm, which rested against the roof of my truck. He dangled the glove a few inches away.

"Nah, I am going to throw it away. But they have these little gloves in dispensers all over town. It's the law. Where have you been? You don't let your dog do his business and leave it do you?"

"My dog normally craps in the woods," I said.

"Oh." He looked confused and argued, "The woods doesn't sound like a good place for a dog. Well, I just wanted to see the beagle, I had better be going." And off he walked, leash in one hand, fresh scat in the other.

I pulled into the church and spread a wool shirt on the passenger seat for Duke to use. It seems to me that no beagle can nap before he fluffs the ground beneath him for a few minutes and then spins in several circles. I locked him inside the cab and walked into the meeting, the grey sky above me and the cold wind whisking long-dead leaves along the snow-dusted sidewalk beneath me.

Just a few minutes into the meeting a frantic woman entered, "There is a dog locked in a vehicle outside! I think it is dead! Who would leave a dog outside in this cold air?"

I ran out of the meeting, and the woman followed. We got to my truck, and I unlocked the door. The sound woke the slumbering beagle, who thought it was time to either go in the house or chase some more bunnies. The temperature was maybe twenty degrees outside, and the dog was snoozing just as comfortable as can be. For some people this just seems abusive. Following the meeting I took Duke with me on a hospital visit. Again, he slept calmly in the seat while I went inside. I let him out, on a leash, to pee when I returned from seeing parishioners. A jogger stopped and admired the young dog.

"Nice coat, who is your groomer?" she asked.

"Pardon?" I answered her question with a question.

"Who shampoos and brushes your dog?"

"Oh," I scratched my head, "my wife shampoos him if he gets into something gross, but for the most part he is washed by dew and rain, and he brushes his own shedding hair crawling through the briars. I pull the briars out at night when we watch the news."

"Briars? Barbaric!" she screamed and kept jogging. I stopped at a nursing home next, and Duke went in to see a few people. He wagged his tail, got his belly rubbed, and made cute faces for a few residents before we turned the vehicle in the general direction of home. We paused for the last hour of daylight at a small tract of land that sometimes yields a good chase. I put the wool shirt and a pair of bibs over my Dockers and dress shirt, exchanged my shoes for Muck brand boots, and turned Duke loose for a chance at one more rabbit. The running was fast and furious, and I rolled one rabbit after just one circle. A second was killed after a long chase that lasted until almost dark. The two rabbits joined the one from the morning, and I picked the scenic route home.

On the way I got to thinking about how good those three rabbits would be for supper the next night, so I stopped at the grocery store to get the ingredients for a little rabbit stew. I ran into a guy I knew from the college campus. "What, did you go vegetarian?" he asked looking into my cart. A shopping cart can indeed tell you a lot about a person. His cart was filled with chips, soda pop, frozen pizza, hot dogs, ground burger, and buns.

"Nah," I said, "Just getting the stuff I need to make a rabbit stew—all I have is the rabbit."

"Where did you get rabbit meat?"

"In brush piles," I said.

"Oh," he drug out the single syllable and raised his eyebrows. "I didn't know you killed things. I never saw you doing that."

"Well, no," I shrugged my shoulders, "that isn't the sort of thing a person does on a college campus."

"You teach philosophy, right?"

"Yep," I answered. "And many fine philosophers hunted, going all the way back to the ancient Greeks."

"I suppose you're right," he said. We exchanged a few bits of small talk, and off he went. I took Duke home, cleaned the bunnies and placed them in the fridge to soak, and drove off to a meeting. Duke looked at me disapprovingly from the couch, feeling that he was obligated to go with me everywhere. On the way to the church I had a startling thought: we are in the minority. Those of us who hunt with hounds are on the outskirts of society. The idea that dogs can exercise in the woods, leave their poop there, stay in shape by chasing another animal, and keep their coats pretty by shoving their bodies through brush is an odd idea to many. Shooting our supper in front of our beagles is even stranger to a world that seems to be convinced that meat grows boneless on cellophane-wrapped Styrofoam. We may well stand at the end of an era, about to go the way of steam locomotives, dinosaurs, and real cowboys. Such things are extinct, or at least very rare. There are novelty steam engines. The alligator is said to be as old as the dinosaurs. We still have Wyoming. We also still have the readers like you! The hunting season is near its end, and maybe I will see you out there on my wanderings and wonderings.

Mud

It has been a nice winter. What I mean by that is we had one. Last year I saw swarms of bugs in the woods every single month of the year, including the traditionally frigid January and February. This year I actually got to wear my snowshoes for a few hunts. Winter was good, and it may have some better side effects. I heard one of the news people say that it may have been cold enough during the polar vortex to kill the ash bore beetle and maybe the deer ticks. I hope that is the case. I spend much of my time waging war on the ticks. A few years ago I had a tick bite me high on my leg. When I say it was high on my leg, I mean that if it went any higher it would have no longer been my thigh. Had it been higher, it would have been in a place only visible if wearing my birthday suit. My upper thigh turned red and was severely swollen. I removed the tick and took it to the ER with me.

"I had this tick in me," I held the little zip-top bag with the dead bug in front of the doctor's face.

"Thanks." She grabbed it and threw it in the garbage.

"Do you want to test that thing?" I asked. "It is a deer tick."

"I don't know what kind of bug it was," she said. "Can you take off your pants?"

"It was a deer tick," I said. "Should it be tested for Lyme?"

"Nah," she said. "We will give you preemptive antibiotics. Could you remove your pants?"

I dropped my britches to my ankles. "Well," I said with seemingly no dignity as my belt buckle rattled against the linoleum floor, "I do worry about Lyme disease."

"Hmmm." She pinched my leg with her gloved hand. "Could you remove your underwear and lay on the bed?"

"I'm in the woods a lot," I said, lying on my back, nude from the waist down. "I often worry if I carry Lyme. I could easily have had a tick bite in the past and never had a rash. I mean, I could have had a tick that drew blood and dropped off of me and never knew it. Should I get tested for Lyme?"

"This is really swollen," she said, ignoring me. "Better get an ultrasound."

Now I was confused. Cripes, was it an alien tick that impregnated me? An ultrasound seemed odd. I quickly stripped naked (well, took off my shirt) and they gave me the backless pajama thing to wear. A really old guy rolled me down the hall. He was a volunteer and was there to make sure that I did not exert myself. The ultrasound showed that I had a swollen leg. Coincidentally, that is precisely what anyone would have guessed by looking at it. I was sent home with antibiotics that would treat the skin infection from the tick and would also prevent Lyme, or so said the doctor.

Ever since that day I have been doing everything I can to stop the ticks. I put the medicine between the dogs' shoulder blades, I spray my clothes, and I wear bug spray on exposed skin. When I come home from the woods I take off my hat, and my wife picks through my head like we are chimpanzees. I then pat the dogs down and look for any ticks that may be present, although the medication that I put on them every month does kill the ticks that attach without my finding them.

When the news said that the subzero air might put a dent in the tick population, I was overjoyed. I enjoyed the cold air as I walked outside with great joy. When the groundhog in Punxsutawney predicted six more weeks of winter, I was happy! I mean, who believes a rodent that should be hibernating anyway? Even so, the cold air seemed like a good idea, and the February snow gave a chance to look for new rabbit spots.

March, of course, marks the end of rabbit hunting, and I will be in the beagle clubs again. I have not been inside the running pens since late October. While the bunnies at the clubs are trickier than the wild rabbits I have been hunting, they are also more plentiful, and long chases will typify spring. I like to listen to these chases as the dogs plow through the muck and brush. The wet ground makes for high scent, and the pack performs quite well. Getting spoiled by good scenting conditions is a big part of spring for me.

And then there is the mud. The ground thaws and makes mud. It rains, and the grass hasn't yet returned, so it makes mud. The snow plows have rearranged the shoulders of the roads, and the result is mud. My wife thinks that mud is the worst thing in the world. The dogs, of course, are covered in mud from their chases. They dry on the way home, and they are simply dusty by the time we enter the house. I still find this to be an amazing phenomenon. When I return from the beagle club and the dogs get excited at seeing my wife, they do a full-body wag. Clouds of dust hover about them as they do their happy dance—sort of like Pig Pen on Charlie Brown. This, of course, bothers the wonderful lady that runs the house.

One time my wife, Renee, decided to bathe the filthy pooches to remove the dust. This turned out to be a mistake, and rehydrating the hounds' coats just turned them into mud all over again. This, too, is a fascinating phenomenon. When she got done with the canine cleaning, the tub looked like an old, dirt road after a torrential downpour. The new strategy now requires my brushing their coats, while sitting on the porch, in order to remove the dirt without water. Each stroke of the brush contributes to the cloud. Soon it looks like I have been cleaning the chalkboard erasers while smoking cigars, if the chalk and smoke were brown. The dust cloud is that large. The porch looks like we live on a dirt road on a hot, summer day after a truck has barreled past.

Then there is the mud that sometimes makes it into the house and is left as footprints.

"You were running dogs!" my wife yelled last year on a March morning.

"Yeah, how'd you know?"

"The muddy footprints!" She held her arms out to her side and raised her shoulders so as to point out the obvious answer to my question.

"I have to wipe their feet better, I guess."

"What are you talking about?" She dropped her hands to her side and squinted one eye in confusion.

"If I wipe their paws better, it will cut down on the muddy footprints," I explained while holding a beagle paw. "I meant your footprints!" Her arms went out, and her shoulders shrugged upwards. "Why don't you wipe those better? Or take the boots off?"

"Oh," I said. I now have to hose my boots off before entering the house and remove those boots as soon as I enter the door so as to let them dry on a rubber mat. The mud, of course, accumulates in the undercarriage of my truck as well. Last year I ran dogs before attending a nine in the morning meeting at a neighboring church. I was punctual and parked in the spot with the sign that said "Reserved for Pastor." No doubt the sign meant the pastor who served that church, but since he was late, I took the spot. I went into the meeting while the mud-covered beagles napped in the dog box. I made sure they had lots of water to drink and went into the church. Hours later I left, and as I backed out of the spot, I realized that clumps of mud fell into the parking spot. Dried chips of clay-like clods were strewn everywhere. I chuckled, knowing there wasn't much I could do to fix the problem, and drove away. Surely, the pastor that works there got the blame.

The worst mud of all is the stuff that gets your truck stuck. A couple years ago, in March, I parked my truck and started running dogs. I was at a spot that I did not want to share with anyone. I had found the location by accident myself while trout fishing. It was close to a nursing home that I go to in order to do pastoral visits. The ground looked quite solid when I parked, but upon returning to the vehicle after running a few dogs, the tires were starting to sink. I tried to get out but just got more stuck. I decided to rock the vehicle by transitioning from first gear to reverse. Even the dogs knew this was a mistake.

I put dead limbs under the truck tires to get some traction and was able to move out of my own ruts and creep towards the hardtop road before getting stuck again. I eventually had to admit defeat and call my buddy Lenny. He arrived with tow straps, winches, and shovels. Lenny was only too happy to rescue me. If it had not been for the fact that I had to get to that nursing home, I would have gladly sat there for days waiting for the ground to dry—Lenny knew right away I was running dogs, and he has claimed it as his hunting spot, too. Oh well, he is a good friend. Now, if you will excuse me, my wife is complaining about the porch. Apparently, the dust I brushed off the dogs has gotten wet in the rain and turned the porch into a mud pit that could swallow a John Deere tractor.

CROWS AND CPS

A couple years ago I was frustrated with the crows. I live in a neighborhood where the pests will open a garbage bag in the twenty seconds it takes to walk from the curb to the front door. The nearby university tried to solve the problem with loud noises. The birds flew away until the noise stopped, and then returned. We now put our garbage bags inside a can. One day I looked back at the garbage before entering the house and saw a crow pull the lid off the can. I reached down, grabbed a rock, channeled my inner little leaguer, and hurled the projectile sidearm. No one could have been more surprised when the damn bird fell to the ground. My aim was true, and there was no shoulder pain. I was convinced that nothing more amazing could happen to me that day.

And then something utterly amazing happened after I walked into the house. Hundreds of crows lined up on the power, cable, and phone lines that lined the two streets that form the intersection where our garbage is collected. And they had a funeral. Wailing and cawing and noises that come straight out of a horror movie filled the street. People walked outside in the cool morning air to behold this spectacle. My wife, Renee, looked nervous. "They are smart, and they carry vendettas," she said, peeking out the narrowly opened venetian blinds.

"They're crows," I said. "Highly social and intelligent, but not the mafia."

"This thing ain't over," she said, and walked to the kitchen to finish her breakfast. Did I mention that her entire worldview is shaped by crime dramas on TV?

The next year I planted flowers, purchased already in bloom from a greenhouse, and a few were plucked out of the ground by crows. I replanted them and walked up to the front door of the house where my wife was watching through the curtain. "They know what you did last summer," she said without opening the door.

"What? I asked. "Can you let me in?"

"Quickly," she motioned, opening the door just enough for me to enter.

This summer my wife lost her cell phone. She remembers putting it in her purse in the car. She remembers walking into the house. The phone was not in the purse the next day. This has caused some problems for us. Text messaging is her preferred means of communication. I often find marital orders transmitted to me via text message. I often leave my cell phone in the truck and do not get these messages, which gets me into trouble. I had a reprieve from these marital imperatives for a day or two, and then I found a gaboodle of texts on my phone when I returned to my truck after leaving a meeting. The gist of those texts was a list of chores I was to accomplish before returning home. I sent one text. It read, "OK. Will do. Glad you found your phone."

About 3.2 seconds later I had a long text message, "I did not find my phone, but I can access my text messaging account through my iPad. Feel free to send texts to me throughout the day, but I cannot answer phone calls. Oh, and I can only receive texts from iPhone users. So feel free to send me information this way throughout the day when I am in the office. In fact, I can text even faster, because I am using a full-sized keyboard connected to my iPad."

Oh, good. Just what I needed. She upgraded to the Gatlin gun of texting. I wasn't going to reply, but she sent another text that read, "I think the crows took my phone. I probably dropped it in the yard when I walked to the house from the car. They probably carried it off. Remember the rock you threw?"

I had to reply. "U R nuts. That's a heavy phone."

"Maybe two or more carried it together. Remember how many showed up for the crow funeral?" I decided to not reply. Despite her ability to text, she has been greatly distressed without her phone. The search continues inside the house, just in case she is wrong. She is due for a phone upgrade this month and will get a free phone then— the newest model.

It has me thinking about technology. I own both an older Garmin and an older SportDOG tracking system. Not long ago I used both at the same time. I stood there looking at both remotes when the dogs were not chasing a rabbit. Just to know where they were. I hear people describing their time afield with the hounds in terms of the average speed that the dogs ran, or the total mileage accumulated in a particular outing. "Come here!" has been replaced with a tone sent via satellite from a handheld remote to a collar.

And I am a fan of this technology. Last hunting season I had a buck rabbit (I killed it to find out this info) run out of hearing and not return. I looked at my GPS and saw that the dogs were circling the rabbit in a whole different area from where it was jumped. I was waiting for the rabbit to return when I looked at the data and realized that the dogs were circling the bunny—several times—over one thousand yards away in another valley. I walked over there and shot the rabbit. Buck rabbits will travel long ways to find females, and this was in the early season, and I think they were still reproducing. It is common for these male rabbits to return to their home acreage and then circle. In the years before GPS, I would spend much time trying to locate the dogs. I would worry that they might be chasing a deer and would sometimes be forced to leave a vest overnight.

There was another day last winter when I got to a favorite hunting spot, and the battery on the tracking collar was dead. I briefly considered going home. Then shame overran my soul. "My father would kick my rump," I thought. Only I didn't say rump. I put bells on the dogs and had a good hunt, killing two rabbits. I have since run bells with tracking collars and have spent many days never looking at the GPS. My dogs hunt close, usually return when they hole a rabbit or lose it, and come when called. They were trained before I ever owned a tracking collar. My concern is that the technology will replace basic houndsmanship. I fear that handling will not be emphasized at all, and we will all be hunting with the club dog. You know the club dog, don't you? The owner has no idea where the hound is at until it starts chasing. It may even be able to run the fur right off a rabbit. It is the kind of dog that makes you run to it when it is chasing. Or maybe it is missing for an hour; and then you hear it, go to it, and shoot the rabbit. It may well have been chasing the entire hour it was missing, who knows?

Current technology allows that dog to be the norm. You may have to be willing to allow for a few road casualties. Here is the thing. I like wool clothes. My favorite shotguns are made from Damascus steel in the early twentieth century. I like my rubber boots to be made from real rubber from real rubber trees. I prefer leather leashes. I own a hound horn and a whistle made from an antler. Oh, and I want beagles that handle well and listen to me. Don't get me wrong, I take the GPS with me, but I am proud of the fact that I can hunt all day and not look at it. Oh, when a buck rabbit runs a half mile, I want that technology available. If I hunt snowshoe hare and the dogs run out of hearing and change to a new hare and run out even further, I will be very grateful for the modern technology. But I do not want to be a slave to a digital screen or fear a dead battery. I have to go. My cell phone has been buzzing like a video arcade. I am sure I have a whole list of marital imperatives to obey. She feels that the bird guano on the cars is a crow conspiracy.

PRO-HUNTER

"I saw a dead pheasant downtown," my wife said to me.
"Wow," I said. "Ring neck?"
"It was a hen, but a small one."
"Are you sure it wasn't a grouse?" I asked.
"Maybe." She closed one eye as if she were straining her memory. "It has been so long since you shot a grouse, I forget what they look like. You shoot more of those game-commission-stocked-pheasants that are too stupid to fly."

Well, if she only knew how hard it is to hit a grouse, she would be impressed with how many I do shoot. I am, by the way, better at shooting them then I used to be, because I have missed so many grouse that I suffer from hearing loss. The thunderous explosion of wings no longer startles me as it once did, and I no longer have to fight the urge to wet myself from fright before taking a shot at the flushed birds. There is the additional defense that I shoot all my game birds over beagles, and this makes it more difficult because the dogs aren't trying to point at the birds. They just happen to bump a few into the air while they pound the briars and brush in pursuit of rabbits. The easiest grouse to shoot, for the record, is the one that senses a beagle moving through the thickets and flies straight up to a tree limb, as if waiting for any other predator to walk away. There may be something unethical about blasting a grouse off a twenty-foot-high tree limb; but when you have been entangled in grapevines and mountain laurel, covered in scratches from trying to swing a shotgun in cover too thick to even walk, and your right shoulder is green from recoil because you aren't able to get a steady mount to your shoulder, you tend to get a little eager to finally hit one of the things. If you account for the cost of ammo that is used in missing grouse, as well as the small size of a grouse breast, you will find that the average cost of grouse meat is approximately $89.50/pound. And that is not counting the cost of gasoline to drive to the grouse coverts. I only took one semester of calculus, and that was a long time ago, so I am unable to tabulate the cost of woodcock meat. Most mathematicians would no doubt say that truffle mushrooms are way cheaper than woodcock breasts in terms of dollars/pound.

Anyway, the important thing to realize is that I was just impressed that my wife knows a few species of wild game. Anti-hunting is increasingly an attitude that typifies American life. I work in a rural church, my wife works in an office at Penn State as well as in a church near there, and we occasionally have people over to visit for supper. Her friends tend to be unfamiliar with wild game. Mine are well-versed. In fact, my friend Lee used to get his kids to eat domestic meat by telling them it was venison.

"I don't like this," one kid said, looking at a pork roast on New Year's Day that was cooked in sauerkraut.

"If you don't like the sauerkraut, you can skip it, but eat the venison," Lee said.

I looked at him, and he put a finger to his nose to hush my question. The kids' eyes lit up, and they devoured the pork. "They don't know what venison looks like," he later said to me. "All they know is that deer meat is a long-awaited treat by the time deer season gets here."

When my wife's friends come to eat, we almost never have wild game, or I can make a side dish or appetizer. Given the fact that the beagles and I do a lot of rabbit hunting, I tend to make buffalo rabbit wings. These are made from the front legs of the rabbits, and they are browned in a skillet and then baked in a casserole dish covered in the wing sauce of your choice. On several instances our dinner guests ate more than a few "rabbit wings" before they realized that they were not eating chicken. My wife usually warns her friends that they are about to eat game, but sometimes she is so busy being a good hostess that she doesn't tell someone before they grab a rabbit leg.

"These wings are shaped funny. Are they whole wings?" one gal asked.

"Sorta," I said. One guy ate a whole dozen and was looking for more until he heard that they were rabbit meat.

They can't seem to get beyond the fact that I killed the meat on the plate, or maybe it is the fact that they know the guy who killed the animals. Perhaps that, more than anything I have experienced as a hunter, explains the world where we hunters now live. It isn't just that there are anti-hunters in the world; it is just a reality that America is a suburban culture. Less and less of us live in close proximity to nature, and almost no one has anything to do with food procurement. People don't even grow gardens like they once did, the preference being for a well-manicured lawn with the grass cut in such a way as to make beautiful, checkerboard sorts of patterns in the yards.

Hunters have been cast in a bad light—just like the rest of rural culture. Oh, there are times when rural life is romanticized like *The Waltons* TV show, but more often than not rural people get caricatured more like *The Beverley Hillbillies*. Did you notice I had to go back a few decades to find television shows that focus on people who do not live in cities or suburbs? By the way, hunting takes place in rural places. I know a lot of hunters that are originally town-types. I won't embarrass any friends by name, but I have taught more than a few people how to butcher a deer. Some of these guys were paying $75 to a guy to skin and butcher their venison. Sure, it is still cheaper than grouse meat, but come on!

Not only are we a city-minded culture, we are an inside culture as well. People don't think about where food comes from—it just appears as boneless meat on Styrofoam plates and wrapped in cellophane. People know the story plots for dozens of television shows and can't name more than a handful of trees. Of course we hunters are one of the few exceptions to this rule. I went through a time period when I did not eat domesticated meat. I was single and did not have anyone to feed but me. I was shooting lots of rabbits, birds, squirrel, and deer.

"Nah, I don't eat beef," I said at a barbeque.

"Because they are a living and sentient creature?" was the response of a vegetarian that was eating a bunch of grilled vegetables.

"Oh no," I said as I grabbed a rare venison steak off the grill. "Because they are stupid. I was hunting rabbits on a farm and watched this cow walk right up to people totally unaware that it was going to one day be food for those people. I decided to stop eating any meat that is too stupid to know that it is food."

I see now there is the paleo diet where you eat like a caveman. I suppose I kinda ate that way for years. It intrigues people. In college I had to give a persuasive speech on a topic of my choice. I decided to speak about why hunting is a great idea. No one cared much about the financial boost that hunting gives to the economy. Even fewer cared about the fact that sportsmen probably do more to conserve land than anyone. They all liked the fact that wild game is healthier than domestic meat. Maybe we have to appeal to the selfish side of people. Do you like seeing wild places that are not yet transformed into parking lots and malls? Do you like healthy protein from meat that lives so freely that it makes free-range livestock look like it has spent life incarcerated in solitary confinement? Are you looking for meat that does not live on antibiotics? Would you be in favor of outdoor exercise that also puts food on the table?

Those of us that train hunting beagles are in the field all year long, training our dogs and shooting a few rabbits in season. We know the smell of approaching rain, the feeling of the air as it cools in the evening and improves scenting conditions, and the rhythm of nature's cycles. Even now this is almost esoteric knowledge to most Americans. A hunter could be defined as a person that advocates a healthy diet, lots of exercise, and conserving the beautiful creation that God gave us. In that regard, I think more people than we think—the ones that do not hunt and live on cal de sacs—could be persuaded to be pro-hunters rather than antis.

BELSNICKEL AND SELF-ESTEEM

I have noticed that when it comes to parenting, the self-esteem of children is a tremendous concern these days. This would be strange news to parents of bygone eras, who seemed to feel that self-esteem was a synonym for pride, and therefore something that should be kept in check. Let me give you an example: when I was in fifth grade I was the ringleader behind a prank, wherein the whole class simultaneously dropped their books on the floor of the classroom in order to startle a substitute teacher—one that many of us were not fond of having in the classroom. Basically, she read magazines all day and punished us if we made noise. She would be in another classroom the next day, and she was basically babysitting. I was very impressed with the coordination and the fact that we all managed to be mostly synchronized with the *WHAP* of our books hitting the floor at once. Of course the note that I circulated to everyone stipulated that we were going to drop the textbooks at the exact second the clock reached the top of the hour. It was a clock with hands, or as my stepson calls it, an antique. Every single kid participated. We were frustrated with sitting still and silently doing nothing. Back then we didn't have our own phones or laptops, so learning was a better alternative to watching a substitute teacher read magazines and romance novels. I did keep comic books in my desk just for days with substitute teachers.

The teacher dispatched a runner to the principal's office, who quickly arrived upon the scene to make sure that the events were not symptomatic of a wider revolt within his prison—I mean elementary school. "Tell me who had this idea, or I will punish every last one of you," the principal said. Quicker than a hiccup, a half-dozen kids stood and pointed at me, including the chubby girl sent to the office to retrieve the warden. I was led to the gallows. The trial was swift:

"Why'd you do it?" he said, holding his paddle.

"She just reads all day and makes us be quiet," I answered.

"Well, bend over and look at the corner of my desk."

One swift swat later I was ordered to sit down, which is somewhat uncomfortable after a swat. I looked up at the principal, not in defiance, but certainly in a way to indicate that it didn't hurt so much that I would react. It was my first paddling at school, and I wasn't sure what was going to happen next.

"You can go back to your class," he told me as he hung his paddle back on the wall. Teachers hung paddles on the wall then, the way a doctor might display a diploma from a medical school.

"Alright then," I said and started for the door.

"Oh, and write a one page paper saying what you did wrong, and have your dad sign it. It is due tomorrow." The principal winked at me. That is when I started crying. Of course I got punished at home, too.

No such event could happen today. Don't get me wrong, I am not advocating the return of paddles, but there seems to be too much focus on self-esteem. When a kid comes home with news of discipline, parents get panicked. Kids hope their parents find out that they got in trouble, which seems odd to geezers like me. A kid might get off the bus and sob, "Mom, I got in trouble at school today for talking in class."

"Poor baby! Are you okay? What happened?"

"I got put in time-out and had to sit in a chair in the corner," they whine with a quivering bottom lip.

"OH NO! You are not a bad person, honey. Here, let's go out for ice cream and then get you a toy."

"Can we get the toy first?"

"Sure, honey, and tomorrow I will call that school. They made you feel self-conscious in that time-out. I won't let them do that again."

In fact, kids get so many toys, that Christmas is no big deal. I know parents who have trouble waking their kid to unwrap presents. The gifts are no big deal, as they are saturated with toys. I am no Scrooge, but this Christmas thing has gotten out of hand. Hey, what we need is a not Scrooge, but the return of Belsnickel. Many people, no doubt, are unfamiliar with this Germanic character. Here in Pennsylvania, he is part of the immigrant story. Of course, we all also eat scrapple, so you be the judge about the merits of the Pennsylvania German tradition of my ancestors. Belsnickel is a grumpy guy who carries a switch and candy. Sometimes he carries small toys. As a kid I never saw him, but we put our boot on the porch on the night of December 5, waiting for ol' Belsnickel to deliver his gifts. If I was deemed a good boy, I got a little candy in my boot. If I was bad, I got kindling for the wood burning stove. Kindling scared me into good behavior until December 25 when Santa arrived. Somehow Santa and Belsnickel work together, but I can't remember how. Santa and Belsnickel even looked similar—wearing furs. It was sort of a good cop/bad cop thing with those two. They may have been kin or something. Hey, the Germans also gave us Hansel and Gretel, a story about parents who abandon their kids in the woods during a food shortage where they meet a blind witch that eats children, so you get the gist of how Belsnickel qualifies as a festive holiday tradition.

Following a trip to the front porch that yields a boot full of kindling, one finds his self-esteem a little low. You just kinda stand there looking at it while your sister puts a rock-hard piece of frozen chocolate in her mouth. Secretly, you hope she breaks a tooth on it. You do feel a little better when Dad says, "Great, I will give you a dollar for that kindling so I can start the morning wood fire." I would go to the store and buy penny candy with the dollar and have about the same amount of sweets that were in my sister's boot. Belsnickel kept entitlement at bay and reminded us that good behavior matters. I only rarely got kindling, as I was more rambunctious than misbehaved. Or at least that is my story. I never really got into much trouble after that one paddling in fifth grade.

I did steal an ornament a year earlier, in fourth grade, but no one caught me. We had a teacher that let us color Christmas tree ornaments. They were wooden and shaped into festive images. I think each of us colored two of them. Our teacher then told us to bring them forward, and she would take them home for her tree. This seemed an incredible injustice, and I stole one. The ornament was a wooden cutout that looked like a kid reaching for his stocking on Christmas morning. I colored his hair yellow like mine, and his pajamas blue to match the ones I had. My hair turned brown as I aged, but it is now returning to a more mature shade of blond. My wife calls it gray, but what does she know? She never even heard of Belsnickel until she met me. Anyway, I shoved the ornament into my pocket, and my mother found it when she was doing laundry. What is this?" Mom asked.

"Ooooooooh." I drew out the syllable to think of an explanation. "That is something I made for you. It is supposed to be me." She loved it and held me tight. Years later, when I was in seminary actually, I told her the truth about the ornament while we decorated the tree in early December during my school break. I was in my early twenties at the time, and she was very upset to learn that her favorite ornament was stolen. On the morning of December 6 I put my boots on to go to the woods for deer season, and there was a bunch of twigs in the right boot. I didn't notice them at first, and it hurt! My mom suggested that the twigs may have been punishment for stealing stuff as a kid.

"I wasn't bad, Mom," I joked. "I was being aware of justice! I was fighting child labor abuse." She smiled. I still like to think that much of my bad behavior is just me trying to reconcile good motives in the face of limited choices in an unjust world. I mean, there are problems in this world much bigger than tree ornaments. I know coal miners who worked for companies that robbed their pensions and then declared bankruptcy, people that work hard and never get ahead, and elderly people who are forced to choose between their medicine and food. I sometimes say mean things if I think people lack compassion. No doubt, I am a bit self-righteous about these things once in a while, too. I probably deserve kindling every year, but I still stick to the theory that I often do the wrong things for the right reasons.

I can't be all wrong either. Guess what Belsnickel brought me this year? I got a custom-made shifter knob for my standard transmission pickup truck. It has a pewter beagle in it. It is very cool. My wife said she saw Belsnickel bring it. She also heard me find it. December 6 is still in deer season. I pulled that Muck brand Arctic Pro boot on and landed the ball of my foot on that ball-shaped shifter knob. Twigs hurt less. I may be a pastor full of shortcomings, but I know the story of Christ, a baby who came to save sinners like us. Merry Christmas!

SACRED WATER OR POTATO CHIPS?

If you would have told me when I was a kid that people would pay money for bottled water, I would have thought you were nuts, especially since many of the bottled water companies are selling plain tap water. No one would have dreamed of buying water a few decades ago. The closest you would come to seeing water purchased was some people driving a few miles to fill jugs from a spring in the late summer when their home wells ran low. Times have changed. My native Pennsylvania has many dead streams and rivers caused by coal mining and other pollutants. We also have a few success stories where streams have been cleaned and now contain thriving trout populations. I live very close to Slab Cabin, a tributary of the more famous Spring Creek, which was successfully reclaimed. The Fish Commission even says that the trout in Slab Cabin are safe to eat in limited quantities, but no one does. We just catch the wild brown trout that populate small streams and release them. Whenever I think of trout sustaining water, I like to remember a special place in Potter County, Pennsylvania.

On top of a plateau in northern Potter County, near the New York State border, you stand in a magical place that looks sort of plain. It is a hilltop, but not even the most impressive in the area. I first visited there as a kid, when my father and I left our beagles (my primary outdoor passion) at home during the heat of the summer in an attempt to catch some brook trout in the cold, spring-fed waters that make for year-round trout fishing. We did quite well, as I recall, but never caught a fish that was large enough to be legal after spending a few hours on a tributary of the Allegheny River. As disappointing as it was for me to not land a "keeper" as a kid, catching lots of hard-fighting native brook trout and releasing them to mature makes for a fun morning. When we got done, we drove a short distance and walked to the top of a hill, and Father said, "Stand still."

"What?" I said, wondering if he had spotted a rattle snake or perhaps a wasp nest.

"You are in a special place."

"If you say so." I looked around.

"When it rains here some of the water runs into the Allegheny River and eventually to the Gulf of Mexico. Some goes into the Genesee River and eventually to Lake Ontario and the Gulf of St. Lawrence. Some forms the headwaters of the Susquehanna and goes to the Chesapeake." He turned around in a full circle to take in the moment, or rather to bask in that place.

"Really?" I asked.

"Yep," he sighed. "I am not sure why Potter County is famous for growing potatoes. This seems more important." I was about fourteen at the time, but I remember feeling the vastness of the world, and was convinced that the grandeur of nature could have its beginning in little, unassuming places, like that spot in the Allegheny Mountains, just a short trip from my childhood home. The unassuming hilltop is in some real way connected to Twain's Mississippi. The Viking visitors were believed to have visited the north Atlantic water that would later be named the Gulf of Saint Lawrence, and the Battle of the Chesapeake, where the French Navy defeated the British, enabling the American victory in the Revolutionary War. This obscure spot in the middle of northern Pennsylvania is known as the Triple Divide and is the origin of three massive watersheds. There are a couple other triple divides of this sort in North America, but you have to go to the Rocky Mountains to find them.

I suppose that for much of the world Potter County is mostly about potato chips, even if they do not know it. Pennsylvania leads the country in producing potato chips, thanks to a potato that is especially suitable (moisture levels, sugar levels, shape, etc.) for making chips. A big part of this success is due to Potter County. When my wife moved to Pennsylvania (before we were married) she claims she went to the grocery store and later commented, "I never saw so many types of pretzels, mustard, or potato chips in my life." That's the German influence. Potter County sells a lot of spuds, and bags of chips are one of Pennsylvania's chief exports and one our culture's great indulgences. I like them with a dip made from wild leeks or ramps.

I have to admit that my favorite fish, as far as cooking is concerned, is perch or walleye. I think they are milder and less fishy. Even so, I make an annual pilgrimage to Pine Creek, which begins at the Triple Divide. I catch two legal trout and cook them before swinging myself to sleep in my camping hammock. I often spend the night where I can hear the water ripple past (frequently cocooned in a bug net) thinking about the Triple Divide, which sends water, eventually, to great rivers—the Mississippi, the St. Lawrence, and the Susquehanna. In the morning I fish until I catch two more legal trout for breakfast before hiking back to my truck and going home.

Not all of the farms in that region of Pennsylvania are for chips. There are two Potter County dairy farms that I frequent in rabbit season. One glorious day last fall I shot my limit on rabbits and spent the waning hours of daylight casting a line on Pine Creek while the beagles snoozed in the dog box in the back of my truck bed. I caught a few trout and then drove home, passing the Triple Divide, and winded my way back to Centre County. The roads were full of gas-company vehicles—hydro-fracturing vehicles, flat beds hauling pipe and drills, even a few trailers where the employees will live for weeks at a time on the job site. The Keystone State is dotted with Marcellus Shale gas wells, and no one knows how badly the water will be affected. Many say it is inevitable that chemicals will get into the ground water. No one knows for sure how many wells we have—not even the state government in charge of tracking such things. I know that hydro-fracking is supposedly not damaging to the water, because the gas industry has said that it isn't. What worries me is that the same message was given to us by coal companies about strip mining. They, too, claimed that the waters were safe throughout the process of extracting the natural resources. Tourists from out of state visit Pennsylvania and say, "My, those hills have beautiful meadows on top of them." The meadows are actually rock strewn areas with insufficient topsoil to grow more than poor-quality grass. They are the by-product of strip mining that deforested the hills, removed the tops, rounded them again, and left them as a ghost of their former topography. In many cases, the process of retrieving the buried coal killed the streams below, at least insofar as their ability to support fish. It killed the insects in many streams as well.

In some ways, I think those of us who actually go into nature are the people that see what is happening. We stand in those "meadows" rather than merely driving below and looking at them. We recognize what happens to trout populations. Much of our American culture sees the outdoors as something to be endured briefly as they walk between buildings and cars. Sadly, I think they are happy if they have something to watch on television, a bag of potato chips, and some bottled water. They may not even notice if the Triple Divide is sending more than water as it serves as the headwaters of three great North American watersheds. Maybe the Triple Divide will one day be just a place on a map rather than a source of sacred waters. Perhaps no one will notice what is happening in rural Pennsylvania unless the water gets bad enough that the potato crop is affected.

GAME REQUESTS

Digital screens are everywhere, and they drive me nuts. Sure, we all use the computer for work and keeping up with things, but I can't believe the proliferation of gadgets. I use the contraptions for work, but I do not do anything on them for entertainment. I recently called somebody to learn how to open a new folder on the desktop of my computer—that is how backwards I am with technology. When people say that their computer crashed, I think that they must be talking about getting frustrated because they can't get the program to do what it is supposed to do, and they kicked over the desk, causing the computer to crash onto the floor. I still think a server error is when the waitress brings the wrong food item. Cookies on the computer, for me, are when I am fighting writer's block and decide to get a glass of milk and some peanut butter cookies to see if they spark any creativity. I recently helped a retired church member learn to use an iPad because he decided to go back to work as a construction inspector, just to get outside and stay busy, and the whole industry decided to go paperless in the few years that he was retired. You know things are desperate when I am your technology guy, because I am forever forgetting how to do the most basic things on the computer.

Of course, we all sing the woes about kids not playing outside anymore. There is an initiative that the nation is trying to get kids to play for one hour each day—not in front of a screen. I can remember when kids ran around and jumped all but one hour of their time awake in the summer. Our parents kicked us out of the house in the morning, and we roamed the neighborhoods in packs, like coyotes that infiltrated a town. No one had to be home until suppertime, and parents didn't care if we ate lunch or not. Mothers bought bread in loaves and lunchmeat in pounds, because nobody knew for sure where we would appear at lunchtime. Every once in a while a mother would be caught off guard as she stood on the porch near lunchtime and saw a thundering herd of kids approaching her home like Vikings ransacking an English hamlet. We would eat and move out quickly. No one left time for digestion, we just poured out the back door and on to the next adventure. My mother kept a dozen jars of peanut butter and jelly in the pantry as a backup in case the barbarians invaded and she was out of cold cuts. There was no way to predict how often we would return to any specific house, it all depended upon where we were at lunch time on any given day. We rarely planned the day in advance, and all plans were subject to change. Nowadays, apparently, it is hard to get exercise for one hour.

I knew things had gotten bad when I first noticed television screens in the headrests of vehicles, enabling the children in the back to watch cartoons. What's more, each headrest has a screen so that the kids won't have to suffer the intolerable misery of watching the same cartoon. They each have their own screen and headphones to keep them entertained. We counted cows as entertainment while travelling in the backseat; and your growing cow population was reset to zero cows every time we passed a cemetery. If we got fussy and argued, fathers thought nothing of blindly slapping over their shoulders at whatever kid could be reached. My dad had long arms and could clip both my sister and me with one brush across the back seat. We immediately got quiet and refused to cry, even if we were in pain, for fear that we would be "given something to cry about."

I certainly would not imply that inflicting physical pain is necessary or proper to parent properly, but I would think that equipping an SUV with more technology than a nuclear submarine so that there is an abundance of movies, cartoons, video games, and music would also be a bad idea. So sure, we all agree that the kids are too plugged into the virtual world, and I am not surprised to see college kids walking in front of moving traffic because they are staring at a cell phone rather than looking ahead where they are walking. The last time I taught a college class I found that the kids paid attention, but they all had cell phones vibrating on their desks, gathering e-mails and texts and missed calls throughout the duration of the class. Why they call it a silent setting, I will never know. Sometimes it sounded like a swarm of stinging insects flying in a wave throughout the classroom.

But adults are guilty of this, too. I even have a Facebook page that I mostly use for beagle related stuff—field trial information, discussing rabbit hunting, and selling my books. The same adults who get angry at their kids and grandchildren for playing too many games are flooding me with "game requests." This is not the typical game request that I receive, and I have received many in my life.

During my unmarried years I became something of a crock pot expert. That was crock pot, not crackpot, which is exactly the term that some people would use to describe me, as I am forever embarrassing myself with hair-brained ideas that just do not pan out. For instance, there was the attempt I once had to equip my mountain bike with a dog box and a handlebar mount for my shotgun so that I could pedal into some primo clear cuts to hunt rabbits on roads where motorized vehicles are prohibited. Long story short, if you have ever had a carsick hound, just multiply it by a factor of ten when you are coasting down a rocky, dirt road and swerving to miss ruts while doing all of this one handed because the makeshift gun rack you put on the handlebars did not work out so well and you have to steer with one hand and carry the shotgun (unloaded, of course) with the other. There was a guy that was bird watching that looked quite confused. Well, he may have been catching butterflies.

All I can say for sure is that he had binoculars and something that looked like a net, or maybe it was just a walking stick. When we passed one another, I was rolling at high speed with a howling beagle in a crate that was strapped to a storage rack over my back tire while holding a vintage A. H. Fox double-barrel shotgun (made in Philadelphia) in my left hand like a knight wielding a lance in a joust. My orange hat was attempting to fall off my head, requiring me to grab it with the same hand that held the shotgun, and the orange hunting vest was desperately trying to fall off my shoulders and lodge itself in the mountain bike's sprocket, which would have been bad. Looking back at the event, I would still describe the look on his face as one that exuded more of a concern for my well-being than a fear for his own, but it is difficult to interpret body language and facial expressions at such high velocities. I certainly feel that it was unnecessary for him to dive off the road and into the weeds. I also could tell you whether he was carrying a butterfly net or a walking stick had he just stood his ground. I would have missed him by at least a foot, or at least inches numbering in the double digits. In my defense, he was hogging the only part of the road that was not entirely ripped apart by ATVs, which are motorized vehicles and clearly forbidden on that particular road. Really, the whole problem is the fault of four wheelers.

By the time I got slowed down, I was another mile down the road, and I could tell that gentleman was safe, because he clearly was yelling at me—loud enough that I could hear him over the terrified beagle howling behind me. The hunting, by the way, was great, and the only difficulty I had was getting the beagle back into the vomit-laden crate to go home. I have not abandoned that crackpot idea entirely; it is simply in need of a design improvement. I had trouble getting that dog back into the crate again, even when cleaned. The primary problem lies in securing the shotgun. Rebel is retired from hunting now, and his pups should not have any hesitation trying the mountain bike crate if I can find a way to more easily carry the shotgun and allow me to ride the bicycle with both hands. Maybe a shoulder holstered .410 Contender is the way to go here.

Anyway, I can cook some tasty rabbit in a crock pot. My most common game request is for my rabbit stew, a recipe so renowned that a young city girl reporter for a Pittsburgh news show ate it while doing interviews of tailgaters at a Steelers game; and despite her aversion to wild game and her knowledge that cute, cuddly rabbits were in the stew, she grinned and proclaimed that it was "really good" on camera.

"Pastor Bob, can you bring your rabbit stew to a dinner at a church?" is a common game request.

"Bob, we are having a family gathering. Do you have any rabbits in the freezer, and can you bring your stew?" is another game request that I might receive.

"Hey, do you still make those chicken wings with the front legs of rabbits?" is a fairly common game request.

So you can well imagine my confusion when I check my author page on Facebook and I am flooded with other kinds of game requests. They want me to grow imaginary farms and crush candy. I plant a real garden with vegetables I can actually eat. Candy crush, for me, is when you put a handful of peanut M&Ms in your mouth and bite down. People ask me to play pet saga. I tell them that I live a pet saga every day of my life with these hunting hounds living in my house. Bejeweled blitz? I just went through de-jeweled blitz where I had my beloved twelve-year-old Rebel neutered to help ease problems with prostate infections.

We should be teaching kids to get away from the computers rather than allowing them to encourage us to use them more. The youngsters are creative and smart, and if we can get them to unplug from the web, they might surprise us. They should be encouraged to apply their intelligence in a productive fashion. One of them might even be able to engineer a better mountain bike design for commuting several miles into the state game lands.

SEASON

There are very few seasons that I can identify. Football, I know, is in the autumn. Basketball and hockey both seem to last all year. Baseball seems long, too. Auto racing dominates the dirt tracks around here in the summer. The local news keeps me informed on these things, because I don't keep records. Hunting seasons, however, are well documented in my life. My calendar lists two things—work events and hunting/beagle related seasons. Last summer the phone rang at the office.

"Hello, this is the United Methodist Church," I answered.

"Yes, we would like to get married," the voice came through the line. "Are you available?" Our church once had a policy that charged money to non-church members to get married in the church. The idea was to limit the people who wanted to get married in the church. The policy was opposed to the sort of folks that invite God to the ceremony, and then promptly forget about matters of faith and personal relations by the time they got to the reception. I got rid of the policy when I arrived, and I only charge couples for the custodial fee for the janitor, since the church has to be cleaned again before Sunday worship. I figured maybe some people would get a bad idea about the church if they felt that we were trying to make money from them. I thought grace had a place here.

"Okay," I said to the bride-to-be, who was a stranger to me. "What is your wedding date?"

"The last Saturday of October," she said. I should point out that that is the first day of rabbit season in Pennsylvania. That day was full on my calendar. So much for grace.

"I am sorry I can't make that day, do you have an alternative date?" I said.

"No," she said, "we already hired the caterer for that day, ordered beer for that day, bought honeymoon tickets, and rented the reception hall for that day. We just need a church and a pastor."

You can call me mean and selfish. You can say that I lack compassion. But this is what I said, "I already have an event that day, and I can't make it." If they were church members, I would have officiated the wedding. But they just needed a church and a pastor. They had no preference in either. Their real preference was for the caterer's food, the booze, the honeymoon, and the reception hall. Wedding season is very much a part of my work life.

But now we are into March and the field trial season. I have those dates in my calendar, or at least the dates that pertain to the beagle clubs where I hold memberships. I am field trial secretary for one club, and that means entering all the pertinent data at the AKC website. The good news is that the AKC has tremendous people to help in this process. The bad news is that you need those great people to get anything done! When they said that the website for Obamacare was terrible, my first thought was, "They must have hired the AKC to design it." It is by far the least intuitive website I have ever used. I can see why there is still an option to mail the paperwork to North Carolina. Even if you live in Alaska or Hawaii, it is still faster to mail the paperwork than to figure out the website. Well, maybe not quite—I am not the most tech savvy guy out there. I downloaded their instructions, and it consumed almost all the memory on my computer. It actually appears that they duplicated each page of instructions from a book and then scanned those photocopies into the biggest PDF file you ever saw.

At any rate, even though I do not go to many field trials, I do attend the ones at our clubs. I like hearing and seeing good dogs; and I enjoy a day where everyone around me is as passionate about beagles as I am. If people who do not own hunting beagles or attend field trials listen to us beaglers talk, they think we are speaking a different language.

"Did you go to a trial last week?"

"Yeah, a long drive for NBQ."

"SPO?"

"Yeah."

"I went to a gundog brace trial. The bye hound won it all."

"Good hound?"

"I thought he skirted a lot. But was a great jump dog."

"How'd you do?"

"My brace mate started a trash run. My dog showed him how to really run trash."

That above conversation is easy to follow—unless you have never run beagles or been to trials. In that case, you may wonder why the dog is jumping, if skirting has to do with chasing female dogs, and why garbage bags are in the trial. So many times the things I want to talk about are either unknown or boring to most people, stuff like scenting conditions, line control, tracking collars, habitat, and shotguns. Field trial season is a good place to kick back on the porch of the clubhouse and enjoy the conversations that I do not always get to have at home, even though my wife understands a fair amount about beagling. She just doesn't care very much.

"Hey, honey," I said to my wife, Renee. "The scenting was weird today. The snow had a frozen crust, and it melted a little bit as the rabbit and dog ran across it. I think it resulted in the scent getting stronger on a back track instead of weaker. I had some serious backtracking today."

"Oh yeah," she sighed in obvious boredom. "I told you it was too cold to go out there hunting and that you would catch a cold."

"Sure, but the scenting was not normal for a cold day either. Those dogs are not backtrackers."

"Yeah. The dogs went the wrong way. That's too bad." She rolled her eyes. "At least you didn't shoot any rabbits, because we have to meet people for supper in a few minutes. Put those stinky dogs away and get changed."

No doubt you can see her indifference to my curiosity about the nature of scent and how complex it is. We could have stayed home and had a fantastic conversation about the physics and chemistry of scent—none of which I know —but would love to speculate about based upon

observation. Instead, I had to try to get out of supper with
her friends.

"Achoo!" I sneezed.

"That was a fake sneeze," she barked, never even
looking at me or offering a blessing. "You won't be sick for
a few days from hunting out there today. You are going to
dinner. Get changed."

No, I like field trial season, if for no other reason than
the conversation and the food. My least favorite season is
when my female house beagles are fertile, or in season. I
have two that still come into estrus, and they never seem
to get their menstrual cycles in synch with each other. My
solution is to keep the one dog that is in season in the
basement while the other dogs get to run around in the
yard and the rest of the house. This, to my wife, is an
affront against all women and everything feminine. So
rather than isolate one dog, I have to carefully make sure
that all the female dogs get out while the males spend time
downstairs in solitary confinement. She says this is fair.
What works better, but not permitted by her, is letting the
fertile female go out and pee in the yard before putting her
in the basement. The males will stay outside all day
smelling her urine and practicing their sexual prowess on
each other, hoping for the eventuality that one of them gets
to meet the eligible young lady in the basement.

I mark their heat cycles on the calendar, but the female
hounds do not consult it. It seems they come into season
every six months, give or take three or four months, and
never both together, except in rabbit season. They both
come into "season" during rabbit season. It is quite
frustrating, really. It is also embarrassing, because if I take
my males to hunt with other guys, they spend all their time
trying to sniff the new hounds and mount them. They have
no shame, panting and smiling at once as I yell at them. I
go over to separate them, and I know that my friends are
annoyed. This lasts until the first rabbit is run. Of course
the problem re-emerges the next day, and every following
day, until the girls go out of season.

The howling is the worst. The males bark all day (while
we are at work, thankfully) until their amorous nature
leaves them mute, or nearly so. Thankfully, the neighbors

do not hear this, and the dogs do quiet down when we are at home to correct them. I went rabbit hunting with two male dogs that had mostly gone mute from singing the lovesick blues, although I did not realize that fact until we started hunting. They ran great, but quiet, and I shot a few rabbits before returning to my truck. A bird hunter was in the area, and he approached me.

"I used to own beagles." He extended a hand to shake.

"Oh, well glad to meet you," I replied, shaking his hand.

"I couldn't help but wonder if your dogs were using proper voice?" He scratched his head. "They seemed very tight mouthed from what I could hear."

"Ha!" I laughed. "They aren't babblers to begin with, but they are a little hoarse since they have been barking at home due to the scent of a female beagle in heat."

"Oh yes," he nodded his head in sympathy, "that can be a problem. Not for bird dogs, they don't tongue when hunting, but I know what you mean."

I was glad to have someone to talk to that understood. "I almost couldn't tell where they were for a long time," I said. "They didn't seem so quiet at home."

"I own a springer spaniel now." He looked down at his prized dog only to see my knucklehead male beagles were trying to mount her. She casually sat down so as to say, "Get away from me you vulgar hounds." I hurriedly put my beagles in the dog box, embarrassed.

"Sorry," I said, looking at my feet.

"No problem, she isn't fertile right now," he said, and we departed as friends.

Rabbit season is over, and I am thinking about traveling to a state that has year-round hunting for a quick hunt. I probably won't though. One of my females will come in season and ruin my attempt to hunt another state's rabbit season. Oh well, it is field trial season. Maybe you will have a seasoned hound out there on the circuit, and I will get to see you.

VACATION

Involuntary procrastination is a way of life for people anymore. I am not talking about the fun kind of procrastination where you avoid responsibility by doing something enjoyable. What I mean is more like getting behind because you have too much to do in too little time. Involuntary procrastination sounds better than being behind. My wife accuses me of being behind because I do not engage in "multi-tasking."

"Whatchya mean?" I asked.

"You only do one thing at a time. Why can't you do more than one thing at a time? When you do laundry you put the clothes in the washing machine, and then you do nothing until those clothes go in the dryer."

"Umm, I actually do a lot of reading until the washing machine finishes," I explained, "and then I read until the dryer beeps so that I can get the clothes out and hang them up right away so that they do not need to be ironed. So I am saving lots of time, actually, because there is no ironing to be done." She mumbled in disagreement and walked away.

Anyway, one of the big involuntary procrastinations in my life is brushing the coats of my retired beagles. The younger hounds get brushed in the greenbrier and the multi-floral rose. In fact, their coats look better than the pooches I see that are owned by people who pay professionals to shampoo and groom their pets. The retirees at Ford's Golden Years Beagle Home do not have the luxury of running as many rabbits as in their youth, and certainly not in the summer when the temperatures are high.

I brushed the old timers the other day with the intention of saving the hair in a bag, as I heard that putting dog hair around the perimeter of your garden will help keep pests out of your vegetables. I started with one of those plastic bags of the sort commonly used in grocery stores, and by the time I was done, I think I had enough to fill one of those fifty-five gallon garbage bags that are sold for autumn leaves after you rake them. Or for the mafia to dump a body in the east river like the movies. I sprinkled the dog hair around the border of my garden until it looked like somebody had inadvertently driven a riding lawn mower over nine rabbits, five skunks, four squirrels, two chipmunks, a groundhog, and a whitetail deer. I mean there was a lot of hair!

"Did you try to tan your own rabbit hides again last winter?" my wife asked, looking out the window.

"No, why?"

"'Cause," she spoke slow and deliberately, "the back yard sort of looks like it did the other year when you tried to tan those rabbit hides to make a big blanket, and then it didn't work, and you threw them all out, and then some animal ripped open the garbage and scattered the rabbit fur everywhere."

"That is hair from the beagles that I groomed, and it is supposed to keep the garden from being eaten by critters."

There was a deer sleeping in the garden the other morning. I am considering this as proof that my dogs are not deer runners, as the smell of my beagles clearly does not intimidate the cervid mind, but rather makes them feel safe enough to tromp down my peppers and take a power snooze after eating the lettuce.

During the shedding season for beagles (January 1-December 31) we utilize any number of devices that use static cling, sticky tape, and vacuum power to remove dog hair from our clothes. When I leave for church, dressed in black, I sneak out the door so the tri-colored canines don't get a chance to jump on me and deposit a fresh layer of white belly hair. August seems to be the peak of the shedding season, and I always find myself getting behind on the grooming. Soon it will be cool enough to let the old dogs chase a little bit—a short rabbit run is enough to brush their coats.

Vacation is also one of those things that seem to suffer from involuntary procrastination. Before you know it, the summer has whizzed past us, and as the imminent school year approaches, we realize that we have not yet subjected ourselves to the annual rite of passage that involves traveling long distances in cramped quarters, seeing sights, and returning home. I will be honest when I tell you that I do not come from vacation people. My dad felt that vacation should be utilized to do carpenter work and make more money than his factory job paid for the week. Whenever we left town for even a few hours he would say, "Let's go, so we can get back." Getting back was way more important than leaving, and if he had his way, we would just skip the trip altogether.

I was fond of vacations, because it meant I got to ride in the front seat. I must have been nine or ten years old the first time that my dad was lost and Mom was unable to read the map. Don't get me wrong, my mother could do a lot of things, but reading a map was not one of them. We were somewhere in the suburbs of Cleveland, detoured by construction, when Dad pulled over, put me in the front seat with the unfolded map, and my mom sat in the back seat. This happened while we were on our way to Sea World, which was not anywhere near the sea, but rather along Lake Erie in the Midwest. Looking back on it, I wonder if a big whale was a good reason to go to Cleveland. I guess not, since they closed the place down since then. Anyway, I felt like a big shot sitting in the front seat. Periodically, this would happen on the family vacation, and was always the most stressful part of the trip, unless you count the fact that my father did not believe in stopping until the car needed gasoline. We scampered to the restrooms while Dad pumped gas.

Vacations for my current family are quite a bit more complicated, because we have house beagles that require care while we are away. One option is to board them at a kennel. If you have ever priced the cost of taking your dogs to a hound hotel, you will find that many of these businesses charge as much to let a pooch sleep on a cement floor as a hotel does to let you sleep in a bed. They charge that rate per night. I actually think you would be money ahead to hire one of the professional gundog handlers who would give your dogs daily rabbit chases and then haul them two states away to enter them in a field trial. The alternative, of course, is to have someone come into the house and let the mutts go out in the yard, relieve themselves, run around for a couple hours, and then return to their crate until the next bathroom break or meal.

This can often work well, and be much cheaper, but the beagles are very good at convincing the hired help that they are harmless pets. Before you know it, the caretaker is convinced that the cute beagles, napping on the couch, will continue to be calm and sedative even if left unattended until the next scheduled sortie onto the lawn. This is all part of the beagles' plan, as they will collaborate and put their superior sense of smell and agility to work the moment they are left unattended. Some of the things we have heard from dog sitters over the years include, "Now I know why you want them in the crate while no one is home" or "Do I feed them their daily meal even if they ate a bunch of stolen people food" or "Never mind that last message, the dogs aren't bleeding. They got into some leftover spaghetti I put in your fridge, and it stained their muzzles red. I'm still looking for the plastic bowl."

An ideal dog sitter should have the attitude of a prison warden and the disposition of a woman whose husband has forgotten their anniversary (I can tell you about it sometime). The experienced caretaker of beagles will be immune to cuteness and will know that the cuter the beagle, the more sinister it really behaves. I suspect kindergarten teachers would be great at watching beagles. The tricky thing is making sure that you do not go on vacation the same week as your experienced dog sitters, because then you are forced to hire a newbie. We are about to have this experience.

"Honey, I don't know what to do!" Renee sobbed.

"What's the matter, sweetie?" I asked in an empathetic way by actually turning down the volume of the baseball game while still watching it.

"You are not paying attention to me or my problems. You are watching that ballgame," she said.

"Not true, pumpkin," I grimaced as the Reds hit into a double play. "I am multi-tasking like you suggested. What's wrong?"

"Well, you know how we are supposed to go on vacation with my mom to see her sister and family in North Carolina here in August?"

"What?" I said, turning off the television.

"We talked about this," she sighed. "I think you were putting a new fishing line on a reel at the time, remember?"

"I guess my multi-tasking skills had not peaked yet," I said.

"Well, we have the dates all scheduled and everything, and our dog sitter can't make it." Her bottom lip pouted out and quivered a little bit."

"Do you want me to call a kennel?" I asked. "I could sell all my shotguns to raise most of the money?"

"No," her lip moved a little more, "the kennels are all full."

"Hey," I said, "if you want, I could stay here and take care of the dogs. If I am already on vacation, I could go to the beagle club for the week and let all the dogs get a good chase. I will just let the old dogs have a short run. I don't want you to miss seeing your family."

"You'd be willing to miss out on our vacation?"

I thought about the long drive in close quarters. I thought about my mother-in-law and the need for pee breaks, the problems that would ensue if the batteries went kaput in my stepson's hand-held, video game thingamajig, and the endless debates that would rage about where to stop and eat, and then the longer conversation after the meal to determine if the food was good enough to warrant stopping there again on a future trip. "Sure, buttercup, I would be willing to miss vacation for you." August is looking better. I should have the shedding well under control by the time she returns from the Carolinas. Hey, I can run dogs while they brush themselves on the briars. I am getting the hang of this multitasking thing.

FREEZER

My wife doles out misery every nine minutes each morning. Myself, I despise the sound of the alarm clock and choose to just wake up early. While people have complained about the cold winter we just had, I am not one of them. It is the hot, humid summer that gives me misery, and so I like to take advantage of these cool spring mornings to take the hounds to the beagle club and let them practice on the professional pen rabbits that seem to play so many more tricks than a wild rabbit. I leave the house before dawn and turn the beagles loose at daybreak for an hour or two of chasing while I work on my weekly sermon.

Oh, the dogs would love to go afield every morning, but there are a few things that interfere with their daily spring romp at the club. First, there is rain. Rain has no effect upon the pooches, but I have arrived at a place in life where I am not willing to stand in the rain. Snow is fine, but a damp drizzle will keep me inside. The beagles, however, are conditioned to run every morning. Pavlov could have proven his point much easier by taking beagles from the house each morning a half hour before the sun rises and driving them to a place with an artificially high rabbit population, as generated by feeding said rabbits and providing optimal cover. Pavlov rang a bell before feeding the dog and was later able to make the dog salivate by just ringing the bell. I have done the same with the act of putting beagles in a dog box that sets in my truck.

The internal clock of a beagle is perfect, and if I am not awake at the time that they are destined to go to the woods, they will simply jump on the bed and let me know. See what I mean by no need for an alarm clock? My wife prefers to sleep until 7:00 a.m. The rising sun is way more effective than the bell. The beagles quickly associate daybreak with rabbits. So if I hear the rain pounding on the bedroom window, I just go downstairs and make coffee. The dogs have to be satisfied just to sit at my feet while I do my writing and other work on the computer. Then, at 6:00 a.m., we begin to listen to the boss of the house as she walks across the bedroom floor every nine minutes in order to hit the snooze bar and then walk back across the room to the bed. This, of course, is all so that she can be awake at 7:00 a.m. I can't help but think that it would be easier to just set the alarm for 7:00 a.m., but this is the process she prefers. Six snooze-bar cycles wakes her just before seven o'clock and seven snooze-bar cycles will make her start the day just after the seven o'clock hour. The dogs and I sit in my study and watch the ceiling as we listen to her walk to the alarm while mumbling words that are cusses, or at least Yosemite Sam-like sounds that should be interpreted as the intent to say bad words. The woman is not a morning person. Occasionally, a dog will sit and stare upwards, tracking her movement with an ear cocked to the side and then produce a hound-dog howl in anticipation of her coming down the stairs. Sometimes the mutts will figure out that we are not going to the woods and then just go upstairs and steal the bed before she can get her full daily dose of snooze bars.

But for the most part, the dogs get to go with me every morning to the field. They love it, and it makes a house beagle a lot more pleasant when they come home ready for a nap. I normally never even hear the alarm clock, because I leave the house before it begins. But spring brings another distraction—trout season. I have to admit that I enjoy trout fishing, and my wife gets very happy when I bring home native brook trout for her to cook. Myself, I am not that fond of trout, unless I am camping and very hungry. I once read an article about the Neanderthals, and it said that archaeologists never found any evidence of fishing technology at Neanderthal sites, which may say something about why they went extinct—they ignored a readily available food source—they weren't smart enough to figure it out. I think this actually points to the intelligence of the Neanderthal, who no doubt ate fish and then said, "Let's just stick to deer."

At any rate, I do eat a few trout, but their real value is that they are great for getting on my wife's good side, which is fortunate, because in order to catch trout, I have to get on her bad side. I leave to go fishing at the same hour that I leave to run dogs at the beagle club. What's more, the beagles do not seem to understand that I am not going to the beagle club. They think I forgot them. Have you ever had someone forget you or have you ever forgotten someone? There is not much you can do about it. I once forgot my wife in a bookstore. Sure, it was close to home, but she still got upset. I got distracted in a book I had found (it was a used bookstore), and I was so excited about making the purchase that I hurriedly put down my money and headed to my truck to take it home. I was about a mile from the book store when my cell phone rang, and I saw that it was my wife calling me.

"Hello?" I answered.

"Where are you?" she asked.

"I'm on the way home, I'll be there soon."

"Well, you forgot me at the store!" she yelled.

"Oh yeah!" I remembered that we had gone to the store together and then went to different ends of the endless book shelves. "I'll be right back!" I hate to think what will happen to my mind as I age.

At any rate, the beagles have the same righteous indignation when I go afield without them. Only they have no cell phones. So they yell, "Hey, jerk! You can't smell rabbit scent! You're too big to get through the briars! Get back here! PLEASE, PLEASE, PLEASE!!" Except we can't understand any of that, and what my wife hears, as I roll down the road towards spring-fed trout streams, is a cacophony of howls, yowls, bawls, and barks echoing through the house. There is no snooze button.

As I understand it, she then goes downstairs in order to attend to the pack of hounds. Unable to think of anything else to shut them up, she gives them dog food. At this point, the alarm clock begins to ring upstairs, and she has to go back up there to turn it off. I am told that this is particularly annoying, because it is a reminder that she is awake too early. I oftentimes return home before seven o'clock, the time she likes to awaken, with a daily limit of trout. I leave the entrails in the woods, but the fish always have their heads when I return. Native trout are not the largest, and I want to have proof that they are legal length in the event that I would be stopped by a fish warden. Typically, the wardens concentrate their time at places where people can walk directly to the fishing hole and cast for farm-raised, stocked trout; as this is where most of the fishing gets done in the spring. I have always said that the first week of deer season and the first week of trout season are living proof that the people who do not hold jobs (by choice rather than difficult circumstance) can awake in the a.m. hours, even if for just a week at a time. At any rate, the fish warden is usually found wherever guys can fish from folding lawn chairs.

When I return, the first thing I have to do is remove the heads. My wife refuses to look at their faces when she is eating them. I suppose eating something while looking it in the eye is the same as telling someone a lie right to their face—not an easy thing to do. There was a time when I put the fish heads in my garden. I had read that the Native Americans would bury a fish in a mound as fertilizer and then plant pumpkin, beans, and corn all around the mound. The corn provided a trellis for the beans, and the pumpkin or squash would provide broad leaves as cover to shade the soil and hold the morning dew. Whenever I buried fish in my garden, however, I got roving bands of raccoons that excavated my seeds before they germinated in order to eat the fish heads, and it did not work at all. No one ever tells you what the Native Americans did about raccoons digging up the dead fish and eating them. Anyway, the heads now go in the garbage. Sometimes, if I am worried about the fish noggins getting overly ripe before garbage day, I will take them to a garage owned by one of my church members and use his large, industrial dumpster. They tell me they do get the stray raccoon track in their dirt parking lots on muddy nights. Some mornings it looks like there was a huge party in the garage parking lot the night before.

I digressed. The trout that I catch are then placed in zip-top bags and frozen. I have to make room for them, and this means cooking the venison and rabbit meat that tends to occupy the freezer. Rabbits, of course, are the mainstay of the freezer. We eat a lot of rabbit meat, and I have found all sorts of ways to cook it. I should say that my wife has found all sorts of ways to cook it. I already knew lots of recipes from my mother, and my wife has learned many more. You could say that we eat rabbit the way other people might eat pork or chicken. It is the "still yet another white meat" for us. It is trout season that brings about all the necessary stock rotations in the freezer. A chest freezer naturally tends to fill from the bottom up. This means lots of rabbits in the fall, followed by a layer of venison, then topped with more rabbits. Of course there is the sporadic grouse, pheasant, woodcock, dove, or squirrel. It is those bottom rabbits that need to be eaten, as they have been there the longest and are at the greatest risk of freezer burn.

The beagles are happy to assist me when rotating the stock. I remove the top layers and then dig to the bottom to get the bunnies from November. I set a big box on top of the clothes washer, which sits next to the freezer, and place the uppermost layers in there. The beagles jump in the air and sniff, apparently hoping I will drop a bag of rabbit meat, which they can then consume as a bunny flavored Popsicle. I then get the early season rabbits and move them to the upstairs freezer that is part of the refrigerator. This being completed, I throw the entire first week's catch of trout on the bottom of the freezer. Let me explain:

Trout on the grill stuffed with lemon, garlic, and onions is one of my wife's favorite meals. When we get to the beginning of small game season, in late October, I will be in marital trouble. Nothing serious, mind you, just the odd late-afternoon hunting trip that gets me home too late for supper or the sporadic all day hunt on a Saturday, which prevents me from doing things like raking leaves or putting away porch furniture for the winter on the exact day she wants me to do that. Naturally, I will repent. I have learned, however, that few things work as well as firing up the charcoal grill on a chilly, autumn evening and grilling some brook trout for her. It just seems to make her appreciate my skill set—hunting and fishing. As we all may know, hunting and fishing aren't always the favorite hobby for a spouse.

So as we progress through the spring, my dogs are confused. Some mornings they get to chase rabbits, and on others I will go fishing, and they will get to eat an extra meal of dog food as my wife tries to settle them down. Every April we seem to have at least one catastrophe where the dogs get the trout heads and eat them. So far there hasn't been any medical trouble from these incidents, but it does give them a bad case of halitosis. I figure those sled dogs eat fish heads all the time, but I would not want my beagles to get an acquired taste for this meal. Hmm, maybe they have actually trained me to go get trout heads for them—an anti-Pavlov sort of thing where the human is trained by the dogs. Nah, I am giving them too much credit. If you will excuse me I have to go. I think I hear the chest freezer opening and no one is in the house but me and the mutts.

SET

When I was in high school one of the more common pranks was to "set" someone's locker. Each locker had two doors—one to hang coats and store other longer items, and another above that to hold books. Setting a locker involved opening a fellow student's top door and standing the books on end so that they leaned upon the door. You had to prop the books up with one hand (so they did not fall out) and close the door quickly with the other, removing your hand at the last second. The resultant gravity-fed joke would be that a classmate opened the door to retrieve books for the next class, and all of the "set" books would tumble onto the ground making a very distinctive sound. It was particularly rewarding if a notebook or folder fell as well, sending sheets of homework into the air like leaves in the autumn wind. That was high school.

I knew the sound the minute I heard it. It wasn't the sound of a set locker being detonated, but rather a set freezer. A refrigerator resembles a school locker—taller door on the bottom, smaller door on the top. From where I sat in the living room, I could almost discern the appearance of the kitchen floor. The gallon bag of frozen trout landed and slid some distance. We were saving those for a night with company and a big fish fry, after I was disciplined by my wife for freezing so many in one package. Quart bags of wild leeks (or ramps) probably tumbled and rested near the refrigerator. There were all those little bags of wild mushrooms that I had picked while letting the dogs chase rabbits at the beagle club. They were dehydrated and then frozen. The last of the banana peppers from the garden were stored in there as well, waiting for rabbit meat after the season opened in order to make my mouth-watering recipe that involves ground rabbit meat being cooked, stuffed into peppers (thawed and warmed to room temperature), wrapped in crescent rolls, and baked. You can find the whole recipe at www.beaglebard.com. Click on recipes. I call it "rabbit in the hole."

"Drat it!" my wife yelled. Only she didn't say drat.

"Oh my," I said in feigned disbelief while entering the kitchen, "what happened?"

"A bunch of stuff fell out of the freezer!"

"I see that." I stared at the floor wild eyed and started putting things onto the table. I had known this moment was coming. I had recently been in the freezer to put a few items away. I closed the door by holding the frozen food upright in one hand and quickly closing the door with the other without pinching my fingers, just as I had done so many times before. I, in effect, "set" my own freezer.

"I was trying to get a roast out to thaw for Sunday dinner," she said. And then she began repacking the freezer in a way that the contents would fit and stack nicely. All of those odd shaped items (like a gallon bag of trout) were rearranged with a precision that only Renee could muster. I ask her to pack the car for trips, too. I haul the luggage to the trunk, and she works her magic. No doubt she is a master of that game called Tetris.

One of the last things to go into the freezer was the peppers. "Nice work!" I said as she stood in front of the open freezer with none of the contents even considering a move. When I put the same stuff in there, the food items arranged themselves into an avalanche awaiting a simple vibration. Thank God for those magnets and seals that contain the disaster—at least temporarily. I never did confess to setting the freezer. She never demanded an explanation or suspected me of anything.

I got to thinking about those peppers and the upcoming rabbit season. Pennsylvania has a lot of beagle clubs, and thirty-one of those clubs form the Pennsylvania Beagle Gundog Association. We have been contacted by the Game Commission to help in a study of the Appalachian cottontail, or *Sylvilagus obscures*. The Appalachian cottontail is distinct from the New England cottontail, and both of them are distinct from the more common eastern cottontail. Both the New England and the Appalachian cottontails are species of concern, as their numbers continue to decline due to habitat loss. The Appalachian cottontail is found at higher elevations and in cover that is more woods than field. I grew up on the Allegheny Plateau where they are more common, and we called them woods rabbits, or sometimes blue bellies. They are often slightly smaller than the more easily found eastern cottontail, and Appalachian rabbits do not have a white spot on the forehead like their similar looking relatives often do. In fact, the Appalachian cottontail frequently has a black spot on the head, near the ears, and the front facing edge of their ears is often black. Sometimes they have a lighter-colored coat, which can reveal little, bluish-colored spots on the stomach—hence the nickname "blue bellies."

Anyway, the game commission wants us to save skulls that look like they may come from the more-rare Appalachian. Also, any rabbit shot at higher elevation, or in the woods and away from fields, ought to be saved, as they may also belong to the subspecies being studied. Each skull should be documented as to where and when it was killed in order to help determine the population range of the more obscure cottontail species. I know where a bunch of these rabbits can be found, and they are fun to chase. Although they are often smaller in comparison to the eastern cottontail, they run very big circles in front of the baying beagles. They are great for fast and exciting chases, often through bigger timber and away from the brushy fields. They are the wilder, mountain-dwelling cousins of the valley rabbits. It isn't unusual to get a chase on an Appalachian rabbit and think, "Oh, those dogs are running fast, I hope it isn't a deer!" These are the rabbits that leave snowy tracks in the mountain laurel and big stands of hemlock.

There was a place close to my home that had these bunnies in abundance—and varying hare, too. That area has been razed to the ground in order to facilitate the extraction of the natural gas that lies within the shale stone deep in the ground of the Allegheny Mountains. Habitat loss is one of the biggest threats to both the Appalachian cottontail and the snowshoe (varying hare) in Pennsylvania. I shoot both, but I worry about the Appalachian rabbit a bit more. The varying hare season is only about one week long, and the daily limit is one hare.

The Appalachian and eastern cottontails are difficult to differentiate until they are dead and you look at the colorations. Even then, a skull measurement may be the only way to tell for sure, which is why they want us to freeze the skulls of rabbits that may well be Appalachian.

There are places in my beloved Alleghenies where I know I can find large populations of the obscure cottontail and shoot some. After all, responsible hunting will not impact the species as much as habitat loss due to suburban sprawl, the building of highways, strip mining, and the building of the necessary infrastructure to gather natural gas from deep shale rock. In the past I have refrained from shooting too many woods rabbits. This year I think I will get some. Maybe if I go into the Allegheny National Forest and other large tracts of public land and find the little rabbit that make such great hound music, it will help enact land use policies that promote more wild places and fewer strip malls. Perhaps it will encourage a mindset that looks more towards the critters and less towards the bottom line of the corporate coffers. Maybe the presence of a rabbit that many did not know exists will be one of the great things that ensure the future of hounds and the future of hunting in a world where each generation produces fewer sportsmen.

In just a few weeks our season will open, and I will visit the wilder paces of Pennsylvania. I can picture those big chases now. Woods rabbits running big, squared-off circles with few tricks for the beagles to unravel, as the dogs' hound song ricochets through the hills in a satisfying echo that sounds like two packs calling to one another across the deep valleys. I will have the chance to see the small rabbit approaching when it is well out of shotgun range as it takes large bounds through mature timber. For now, however, it is still time to condition the hounds. They have been running a lot more as the summer heat recedes, and so they are eating a little more, too. On Sunday they may get a little leftover gravy from the beef roast that Renee is thawing for dinner. One thing is for sure—there will be questions that I must answer if she decides to thaw some ground beef and bags of rabbit skulls come tumbling out of that freezer.

FOOT

Put beaglers in a room together, and the topic of foot is bound to come up. As in, "How much foot does your dog have?" This is a perennial question and one that I think has to be viewed with a bit of skepticism—fast to one is not fast to another. I got started with beagles in the 1980s in Pennsylvania, and while the Large Pack format always has featured hunting hounds, the same can't be said for many Pennsylvania beagle clubs. SPO trials were not common then, and the clubs that did hold field trials catered to the traditional brace crowd, who ran beagles that looked more like bassets. Well, I take that statement back as it is an insult to aficionados of the basset breed. These brace beagles were bow-legged, ponderous beasts that looked like old, wooden barrels after the steel hoops gave up their structural integrity. My dad and I had the only hunting dogs in our beagle club. Those brace guys would run their dogs to "take the edge off their hounds" before a trial.

Now, I know what you are thinking. For us gundoggers this means letting the dogs get a long chase to settle them down a bit for the next day. Maybe the dog is a little mouthy if it isn't run every day, or maybe the dog gets so excited that it gets a wee bit rough if not run hard. This is what we like in a dog—desire! These are the dogs that can hunt all day. This is not the case for those brace boys! I watched them let the dogs "run" on a marked line for forty yards. It took ten minutes, I am not exaggerating. They sometimes carried lawn chairs (not at their trials, but during "training") that they could sit on to watch as the beasts bellowed and bawled, their baying blasting the grass-like palm trees in a hurricane as they tongued two, three, or even four times before taking a slow, single step forward. They never ran more than two dogs at a time (brace, I know), and I am not sure that the second dog was barking on rabbit scent—it may have been using its voice every time it smelled the breath left on the grass from the hound in front. And it was always on grass. They walked the mowed paths of the club and waited until they saw a rabbit hop away. The guys at the club called my hounds wind splitters, and I wore the insult with pride. They tolerated my hunting dogs as I was young enough to cut brush, fill rabbit feeders in the winter, and work at the trials. There was a man in my childhood club that would pay me money to have my dogs find a rabbit and chase it onto a path where he could put his brace dogs on the marked line. He was a lawyer, as I recall, and he paid a lot of money for this service.

I would then catch my dogs and move to the other end of the club to get a chase. He would run all his dogs in this way—maybe eight or ten of them, and "take the edge off of them." When I asked what he meant, he said that he wanted the dogs to not shake their head from side to side, but to just place the nose in each invisible footprint from the rabbit and bark until it figured out exactly where to put its nose next. I always told him that my dogs had to circle the rabbit before he could have it, because I was practicing for hunting season. This annoyed him, but the alternative was for him to whack at the brush with a stick until a rabbit emerged, so he tolerated my stipulation. How often does a guy win a disagreement with a lawyer?

Running in a pack brings the idea of foot to a sharper focus. While I have never understood the desire that some people have to throw a blanket over a pack of dogs to prove that they are the same speed, I do understand that a pack that is very mismatched (in terms of foot) will not remain a pack long. We have all seen dogs lagging way behind and barking on scent that is a hundred yards behind the pack. And while I agree that a hound should be able to gear down in poor conditions, they should also have the ability to pour on the pursuit in ideal scent! In the last several years I have started evaluating foot a little differently. A dog that putters and crawls is obviously not fast, but neither is the beagle that launches itself down the line and then shortly makes me wonder if he has solved a four-minute check or jumped a new rabbit.

I once attended an SPO field trial where every dog that could solve a check was picked up for being too slow. As dogs were eliminated, one at a time, from the packs in first series, the chases began to break down until the remaining hounds in each cast were leashed by their handlers and the next pack was judged. The winner's pack was given more rabbits than I can remember and never circled one. The judges kept saying that the bunny had gone in a hole. I may have believed that one or two did, but they were given many chances. I stopped counting on rabbit number ten. Surely one of those rabbits would have stayed above ground, wouldn't it? After all, it was the winner's pack. Blazing speed that results in over running the check can turn into being classified as slow very quickly.

And this has me worried, because there are some who would see foot and the inability to circle a rabbit as being in a causal relationship—as if speed causes the loss of the rabbit. I am not at all convinced that this is the case. Dogs that cannot solve checks come in all speeds, just as dogs that always seem to solve the rabbit's tricks come in all speeds. Beagles of various degrees of foot can jump rabbits well, and dogs that have strong noses come in all speeds as well.

So I think about foot in terms of how long does it take a beagle to circle a rabbit? I am primarily a hunter, and this is what matters to me. I have hunted with dogs that keep the rabbit going with very few checks, but would leave my muscles shivering and my teeth chattering as I awaited a shot on the bunny in the winter—at a certain point, you feel like you are on a deer stand, it takes so long. I have also hunted with dogs that were equally slow in terms of circling rabbits, but they repeatedly lost the quarry by overrunning the line with fantastic speed, and then took many minutes to jump a new rabbit, moving further away and forcing the hunters to move in that direction only to have that chase end just as quickly, after another one hundred yard dash/chase. As a hunter, I value circled rabbits.

One of the blessings I enjoy is the ability to hunt the last hour of daylight on many days of the hunting season before going back to work for evening meetings. When I

only have sixty minutes to hunt, I need circles! So I
propose a new metric for evaluating foot, even if it is one
that doesn't have any bearing on trials or the rulebook. I
evaluate foot in terms of minutes per circle. In other words,
how many minutes does it take for that rabbit to get back
to the gun after it is jumped? Sure, I know the rabbits vary
in the size of their circles. Yep, it is true that the cover may
dictate the running areas of any particular rabbit. But we
all know what a good hunting dog is doing. We can hear
the voices in the pack as they begin to get louder, signaling
that the pack is on the way back. That is when I get statue
still and move only my eyes as I look for the rabbit.

I want the dogs to drive the rabbit, going as fast as they
can but as slow as they have to in order to keep the chase
going. I sometimes worry when I hear too much emphasis
placed on negative judging and looking for faults rather
than merit. I know people who are reluctant to keep a
lemon or red colored beagle because they are easily
noticed. The concern isn't that the merits will be noticed,
but rather worry that a mistake will easily be seen when
the transgression is made by a dog that has a unique
physical appearance. Blending into a pack and not making
mistakes becomes more important than chasing well.
Faultlessness, sadly, is sometimes more prized than merit.
Accomplishment over style ought to be our cry. Sometimes
conversations on this topic can be exhausting.

"That dog shouldn't run over the end of the line at all!"
a radical will say.

"If the dog is running hard, it is bound to run over the
end sometimes," a voice of reason might reply.

"It just can't be too far over the end," another opinion is
voiced.

The discussion then goes crazy, with debates raging
over just how many yards or feet over the end of the line is
an acceptable distance. I half expect to see guys with range
finders and tape measures at beagle clubs, as they will
bicker about the allowable overrun until they disagree by a
matter of a few feet. I tend to get scared when I hear style
overemphasized, because I grew up in Pennsylvania and
remember the brace days, where many of the clubs got so
excited about style that they were putting ribbons and

championship titles on dogs that were unable to find a rabbit or circle it. Thankfully, the gundog clubs outnumber those traditional brace guys now, but I am ever mindful that there was a time in my home state where the term "AKC registered beagle" was a phrase that would send many hunters running. Hunters who did run AKC dogs were frequently getting them from the Large Pack guys to our north, who never forgot that the beagle is a hunting hound.

I for one would like to see AKC pass a requirement that after a beagle gets the necessary wins and points to become a champion, it would then have to find its own rabbit and circle it solo. This seems like an odd thing to say, and something that might seem odd to the originators of our sport. Who would bring a beagle to a trial that can't run a rabbit? In hunting season we encounter guys with packs comprised of specialists—one or two dogs that can jump a bunny and several others that can hold the line. Separately, none of them may be able to circle a rabbit to the gun, but together they can do it by committee. That makes sense for a backyard beagle, but not for a champion. Just think if each newly minted beagle field champion had to find its own rabbit and then circle it all alone. This would spell the end of traditional brace, but it would also be bad news for a few gundogs that follow their owner or handler until the rest of the pack starts a chase, or the prized jump dog unable to consistently solve checks. This simple test would prove that the hound has something to contribute to a pack and remove the focus from foot, placing it on the ability to account for game. And if the beagle already has three wins, it should be an easy test.

Slobs and Snobs

There are a couple things, on opposite ends of the spectrum, which hurt the cause of hunting. I am talking about slobs and snobs. Slobs are fairly common where I live. I am not talking about a guy with his shirt untucked, muddy knees, a mustard stain on his sleeve, and dog hair plastered to his clothes. That slob is me. No, what I mean by a slob hunter is the person that just plain gives a bad name to hunting. In extremes, these guys are criminals—three men were just arrested for shooting bull elk illegally here in PA, where great efforts by the state have yielded a herd large enough to hunt—in very limited seasons with a few licenses issued per year. There are other slob hunters, though, that are perfectly legal. There are guys that just like the thrill of the kill. I have known guys that shoot a deer every year and throw out the uneaten venison from the previous year to make room for the newly acquired meat.

My doorbell rang one day last autumn, and I was greeted by a friend that extended his hand to give me four grey squirrels. "Here, you eat 'em dontchya?"

"Uh, yeah, I eat squirrel, why?" I grabbed the dead rodents by the tails.

"I felt like hunting, but I am not a fan of squirrels," he said, glad to be free of the arboreal mammals that were dead enough, but neither field dressed nor skinned. That sort of an attitude doesn't do much to promote hunting in a culture where a few of us are passionate supporters of hunting, another small group is very opposed to hunting, and most people are fairly indifferent but easily persuaded by the extremes. I have watched beaglers shoot rabbits that are mere feet in front of a dog and seem to have no problem with that type of slob behavior. It is one of the primary reasons that I hunt rabbits with just my own dogs and no other people—or with like-minded beaglers who also refuse to shoot rabbits on the jump.

I am not a big fan of taking shots that are beyond the hunter's skill level. I am an advocate of long-range shooting when it is ethical, but far too often I see guys tracking a deer into the darkness with a flashlight because they launched the arrow from their compound bow at sixty yards and wounded the majestic buck that they wanted so badly. We can promote hunting as an ethical way to get healthy sources of protein. That is a good way to recruit future hunters as people decide that they want to live closer to the land and get involved with their food while it is still living. Every time the news features a poacher or a hunter gets in a wreck due to drunk driving as he left deer camp, we hurt our cause. When some city slicker shoots a dairy cow or horse in a field at first light, it is the sport of hunting that gets the blame rather than the slob hunter that is at fault. What does it say about our culture when people lock up their black labs in bear season for fear the dog will wander to the edge of the woods and be mistaken for a trophy?

Oh, and in full confession, I like to kill animals even though I love listening to the dogs chase more. I would much rather have hours of great chasing and no dead rabbits than a game vest full of a daily limit and frustrated dogs that performed poorly. Last year I hunted cover so thick I could hear the approaching cottontails, but never saw them for the first two days of the season. I loved the hound music, but I was more than ready to put some hasenpfeffer in the freezer! In other words, I admit that the kill is part of this whole thing, even when it comes to rabbits, which are pretty easy quarry with good dogs. The slob hunter has no appreciation for much beyond the kill. The chase, the dogs, and the companionship of like minds are beyond the slob.

On the other end of things, we find snobs. I was in the field last year with a "bird-dog beagle." My old Rebel is a beagle that has always been good for hunting pheasant, grouse, and woodcock. He flushes plenty of each. He will pursue them until he bumps into rabbit scent, and then he ignores the feathers. I blame the bird feeder that was in my yard when he was a puppy. But I like it! I had him in a swampy bottom that is good for rabbit, but better for woodcock. I was hunting both, of course, when I met a guy that looked like he just stepped out of the Orvis catalog.

"How are you?" I asked.

"Fine," he said while fumbling with a lanyard around his neck.

"What's the stitch counters for?" I wondered aloud to him as I saw the focus of his attention, the plastic counting tools strung onto a lanyard with a whistle beside it.

"Pardon me?" The guy stood straight and looked at me. "Sit," he ordered with his pointer.

"The stitch counters." I pointed at his lanyard. "That is what you have there. Two of them."

"These," he annunciated slowly and loudly as he held the lanyard so I could see it, "are flush counters." He paused longer than one would think necessary between the words "flush" and "counters."

"Oh," I said.

"They are utilized to count the number of flushes that one finds when one is on a hunt." He looked down at Rebel, who was rolling in something nasty a few feet in front of the pointer that was still sitting perfectly. "Something you and your mutt clearly would know nothing about. I have one for counting woodcock and the other for grouse."

"I don't know much about flush counters," I said, "but those are definitely stitch counters. My gram used them for knitting or crocheting or one of those things. You can go to a fabric store and ask for stitch counters, and I guarantee they will give you a plastic, barrel-shaped doohickey with moving numbers on it just like those two that you have threaded on that lanyard around your neck. How many birds you kill so far?"

"None yet," he said, "but I have flushed two woodcock and a grouse."

"Good thing you have a counting device for that sort of higher math," I said as Rebel started chasing a rabbit. "I am going to have to get going here now, but I want to show you something." I pulled two woodcock, a grouse, and four doves from the right side of my vest and put them back inside. "Perhaps," I continued, "you may want to get a third stitch counter so you can keep track of doves, too. Maybe buy a beagle to get better results as well. I have to go now, because I already let that old, senior-citizen dog chase two rabbits to the gun today, and I have to go shoot that third bunny and take him home before he gets too tired."

I guess I was a little bothered by his disdain of beagles and maybe even a lot prideful in explaining that his flush counters were actually stitch counters. As much as the slobs bother me, the snobs would be all too happy to make hunting a pursuit appropriate to the leisure class alone. Oh, I confess to spending too much money on gear, and I likewise enjoy the nice stuff. Fine knives, handmade boots, vintage shotguns, and the newest GPS dog-tracking technology can all be found at my home. My shotguns are all used and all scratched, however. I accept briars as part of life, and in many ways the materialistic tendencies of hunting, at least for me, are due to a sense of stewardship. I save money by purchasing good equipment that lasts for a lifetime.

For the most part, our beagle magazines are about local guys that compete close to home in field trials and hunt hare or rabbits even closer to home. As you read *Better Beagling*, or the other beagle magazines, you are reading a magazine where the readers are responsible for most of the advertising. Our clubs advertise our trials. The owners of the most successful male hounds have pages devoted to their stud dogs. Beaglers write about their experiences in field trial competition or hunting. In other words, we are unique in the sense that our magazine primarily features the readers and events easily accessible to the readers. When you look at many of the large distribution hunting magazines on the shelves of bookstores (I almost said newsstands by accident, and I haven't seen one of those in years), you see a magazine that in some ways has little connection to the folks buying them. There are a few "how to" articles and then a lot of stories that feature expensive hunts beyond the financial reach of most guys. The advertising all caters to canned hunts, where a successful hunt is determined mostly by your tax bracket—can you afford the hunt?

The beagling world is a small one, indeed. It is getting smaller with the Internet. When I see a field trial advertisement, I very often know the judges that are listed for the event. When I see the name of the president of the local club, I know what he or she looks like. When the trial lists a phone number for the field trial secretary, I can remember how the voice sounds on the other end from previous phone calls. The beagle magazines truly are a magazine of, for, and by the subscribers. The writers are beagle owners. The publishers are beagle enthusiasts. The advertising is trials that we attend and stud dogs that we have seen!

All of this is my long way of saying that we are part of the backbone of any movement that would prevent hunting from becoming a hobby that belongs strictly to the wealthy. Many of the well-known, national hunting magazines may as well begin with the words "once upon a time" and end with "happily ever after," because they are full of fairy tales. Their pages are filled with commercials and stories devoted to African safaris, guided Alaskan bear hunts, birds in Britain, and other fantasies that are beyond my grasp. Our beagle magazines, by contrast, feature beagle clubs—many of which I have seen. They list people I know. I see the names of dogs that have beaten my own in competition. I have met the AKC representatives, the dog food sponsors, and the folks that make collars, leashes, and other gear. A Maine hare hunt and an Alabama swamp rabbit hunt, while not cheap, are within my budget on occasion. We are the guys that prevent snobbery. Oh, and if you need a "jump counter" to remember how many chases your pack had in the field, I might be able to find one in my gram's sewing stuff.

O'BEAGLE CARE

Getting older is one of those things that creeps up on us, and we don't realize it is happening. I have no real complaints, yet. I know that not too many years ago, when a beagle club was preparing for a field trial and we unloaded dog food to feed the hounds, I carried four bags of dog food at once, each weighing fifty pounds (one on each shoulder and one in each hand) and I am now content to carry one bag on each shoulder, and that is all! But otherwise I feel pretty good. My hearing may be diminished a wee bit from the shot gunning, but, to be honest, for every time I can't figure out a word that I wanted to hear, there must be a dozen pointless conversations around me that sound like nothing more than Charlie Brown's teacher, and it is almost a good thing to hear less—almost.

And being middle aged has advantages. For instance, I can both write in cursive letters and read them. Many high school kids cannot, and in many locations they no longer teach this skill to students. The ability to type on keyboards is viewed as much more beneficial, and the curriculum concentrates on that skill set at the expense of others. I can also read a clock that has hands rather than digital numbers—an ability that seems as fantastical as reading Latin to youngsters nowadays. Being a little bit older isn't all bad. This knowledge may be helpful someday when we are living in nursing homes with today's kindergarteners taking care of us. We can pass notes in cursive writing to one another, plotting our subversive activities. They may as well be Egyptian hieroglyphics— they will never figure out what we are saying. Jail break movies will not be nearly as exciting as real-life, cinematic blockbusters about geezers escaping the shackles of institutional retirement in order to go hunting for a day. As soon as we make it to the woods, they will stop pursuit, as the outdoors is something that they do not enjoy, but rather tolerate in small doses between buildings and automobiles. But, like I said, aging has not been bad for me—yet.

It is the aging of my hounds that makes me resent father time. I love those years when a dog may be just a wee bit past his physical prime but his brains and experience make him better than when he was young and muscular with all-day endurance. They are at the nexus where physical skills are starting to wane, but their rabbit wisdom has peaked. No trick is too much for them, and losing the rabbit is a rarity. This seems to be the years of a dog's life when I shoot the most rabbits over any given beagle. The veteran hounds and I know each other well, and we can anticipate what is going to happen. I can tell by their voices how the chase is going. My ear easily discerns if the scenting conditions are difficult, or if they are so close that they can see the bunny.

Then, in the years that follow, that muzzle turns gray and the pace slows, and before long, the old dog is the only one who hasn't figured out that he just isn't quite the same anymore. It is at that point that I run the beagle solo so that it doesn't have to compete with pack pressure from the younger dogs. Hey, there is no sense in making the old timers feel beaten by youth, or resented. These are the hunts afield where I take my light .410 and only shoot the rabbit if it is getting dark or the dog is tired, and then we go home. There must be some dignity in the aging process. The old timer then sleeps on the couch and has rabbit dreams for the night. Like all retirees, the dogs need special care.

The news is awash with arguments over healthcare—the cost as well as the problem with government involvement and legislation. The debates rage over who has quality healthcare, who does not, and what responsibility employers have in regards to paying doctor bills. The term entitlement gets thrown around a lot. From my perspective, the best healthcare available is the healthcare given to any dog that chases rabbits for me. Entitlement describes their lives, indeed. A quick perusal of my bank statement will bear this out. I don't want to even add the financial totals for medicines fighting ticks and preventing heart worm. Oh, there is the occasional cut ear that requires stitches or a porcupine quill that cannot be removed by me and requires veterinary attention. Prenatal care is present as well. I don't breed many litters, but when I do, I go all out. Two of my females had litters born by C-section. I have a few dogs that have tested positive for Lyme disease, which requires the occasional prescription of antibiotics.

I have a geriatric home for beagles. I have two beagles on Purina NF, a dog food for dogs in kidney failure. It works, as the beasts have been eating it for a couple years and are managing to stay relatively well for old dogs. It is $50 for eighteen pounds and must be purchased from the vet with a prescription. Meanwhile, I am buying groceries in the "buy one get one free" section. I got a blind dog with glaucoma, and the eye drops for pain are not cheap! Degenerative disks in the back after years of plowing through the brush have affected a few hounds.

Sometimes the conditioning of my young hounds takes a backseat to letting the old timers have a brief chase. It is sort of like when they have a baseball game for the retired greats of America's pastime, the velocity is not there on the fastballs, the reflexes aren't as quick in the infield, and the power at the plate is not quite what it used to be either. But I try to let the retirees at Ford's Golden Years Canine Care get a chase once in a while, just enough to let them remember who they are. These outings have a cost too—dietary supplements for their old joints.

Of course there is always the annual physical, even for those young hounds that are fit as a fiddle and strong as a horse. I was at one of these visits recently when the vet said, "This poor guy needs his anal glands expressed," as she stuck a finger up Duke's rear end.

"Oh," I said. "Yeah, I see that now." The goo ran out.

"You know," she said, "you could learn how to do this."

I thought about the cost of draining the dog's butt and put it in perspective of the overall healthcare plan that I was funding. It is a pretty small expense, really. Oh, and my vet treats me very well. She lets me make interest-free payments on the expensive stuff. She is on call for me whenever I might have an emergency, and she has been a best friend at the times when a beloved hound is ready to pass on into the next world. She gives me great service and discounts. Oh, and she has a kid in college, which we all know costs money. So I watched her remove the gloved hand from Duke's rectum after draining the glands and decided that the expense for that service was not so bad.

"Nah," I said, waving my debit card, "I think I will let you do that. He already gets mad enough at me when I take his old dad to chase rabbits instead of him. I think he might resent me more if I did that to him."

AFIELD

Have you ever hung out with somebody that claims to be able to discern what is going on in a rabbit chase without watching it? Do you have friends that are tailgate beaglers? In order to be in full disclosure, I need to admit the following: I sometimes sit still and listen to a great chase. I don't try to follow the hounds, and I don't try to get in front of them to see the check work. Sometimes, I sit on my tailgate and just soak in the sounds. I especially like it when you get a resounding echo that rolls off the hills and almost gives the illusion that two packs of hounds are singing to each other across the valley. I hope those of you in flatland states have some sort of topography that gives you this fantastic auditory experience.

Anyway, having given you that full disclosure, I also want to say this: I have limited knowledge of what is happening in the pack while I listen to a rabbit chase from my tailgate. Maybe the dog to bark first is the one getting the check, but maybe it is a hound barking in the check area and does not have the line. Perhaps an older veteran is solving a trick and running mute for a little ways to steal the front from his younger competition. A screaming chase with no breakdowns might really be due to the fact that there are so many rabbits, that the dogs keep changing from one bunny to another in a seamless fashion, giving the impression that they are relentlessly pursuing one lone rabbit in a determined manner that sounds like a perfect run!

This is why I like to watch a chase. I like to know what faults my hounds are exhibiting, and I like to make efforts to improve those dogs, or at least stop the bad habits that I can, and encourage behaviors that will improve a hound's rabbit-chasing ability. I was recently amazed to hear a guy say that a beagle he owned got most of the checks because a friend of his divined this knowledge from a GPS collar.

Granted, I am no GPS expert, but I can only determine a hound's average speed, total distance travelled, and current location with my GPS. I suppose if a pack of beagles were all wearing a tracking collar, and they all ran the same rabbit for the same time period, you might be able to tell what dogs were exhibiting more line control as they would have less mileage on the collar—the dog that ran a greater distance during the hours the pack was chasing was also running over the end of the line on the checks, and the dog with less miles was more efficient and solving the checks—maybe. On the other hand, if the dog with more mileage acquired that extra distance by running over the end of the line and then immediately stopping and returning to the point of loss and solving the check before the slower dog arrived, then that would tell an entirely different story, wouldn't it?

And here is an amazing thing about watching our own dogs chase rabbits—we can learn to tell what they are doing right and wrong by watching them do it, and then later we can almost visualize what they are doing by the sounds of the chase. If I watch them chase, while listening, I can later simply listen and sometimes guess what they are doing (though not with 100 percent accuracy by any means) based on these previous observations. I had a dog that notoriously backtracked from a hole. I could hear her do it, and it would make me grumble. My old Rebel clucks like a chicken when he is on grouse, woodcocks, or pheasant. Duke squeaks on a cold trail that is not quite fresh, but will have a rolling bawl on hot scent. When the dogs are on a sight chase, Hoss's voice will not be heard, but he is almost certainly at the front of the pack—for some reason he is mute on those instances as he tries to catch the rabbit. No doubt you can identify the idiosyncrasies of your dogs as well.

We are into the field trial season now, and I always feel a little bad for judges. They have to learn the dogs' voices and associate them with collar colors assigned in each pack so that they can score them. These two evaluators of canine ability have no idea what any given dog's peculiarities might be. Isn't it always the case that when your dog is doing well it is never in front of the judges, but rather in the thickest brush pile on the entire running grounds? Oh, and if your dog would commit a mistake, it would happen on the mowed path in front of the judges, the marshal, the gallery, and yourself.

I once made winners' pack on a chase where my dog looked outstanding in second series. She was backtracking from a hole, and I knew it, but the judges did not. On another day, I had a dog picked up in winner's pack for being the only dog not chasing the rabbit. After he was ordered up and eliminated, it was determined that the pack was having a stellar chase on a groundhog. I used to feed rabbit hearts to my beagles. A pack was tested for gun shyness while the dogs were at a loss (I am not sure why they fired the gun then) and Lady ran out of the brush and jumped on the field marshal's leg, looking for a dead rabbit. She was eliminated for gun shyness, when in fact she was harking to the gun. She had learned to associate gunfire with two possibilities: (1) a dead rabbit and a tasty treat, or, just as likely, (2) a marked line where I missed the rabbit!

Have you ever been in a department store when they open the doors for shopping on the day after Thanksgiving? Ever seen the shoppers running up and down the aisles of the store looking for the bargains and sales that most interest them and their plans for the perfect Christmas morning? That is precisely the way my hounds will look for a rabbit in a beagle club—they will cruise the feed strips, running with their heads in the air, nostrils flaring for evidence of a chubby pen rabbit that was recently eating clover on the paths, eyes fixed straight ahead, hoping to see a puffy tail bobbing up into the air. It is downright embarrassing to have people see this at a field trial, especially when the expectation is that they will plow into the briars and bounce a bunny from the bushes. I might want to explain that they are merely employing the strategy that works best in a pen, but I usually just stare at the ground hoping for the best. My dogs are used to entering a beagle club at dawn when the rabbits are all feeding on the mowed paths and are easy to find. They don't understand that the first four packs already made enough noise to chase all the club rabbits off the grassy feed strips.

Meanwhile, my dog is going up and down every path like a shopper in the grocery store before a holiday picnic.

It is no use explaining that the dog acts quite differently in the wild during hunting season where there are no groomed, grassy paths. "Why is he not in the brush?" a person says.

"You know how people eat the wrong food on vacation?" I ask a question in my reply. "And they might wear weird clothes that their friends back home would laugh at? And you know how vacationers take pictures of things that the people who live there would never find interesting?"

"What are you talking about?" the guy might say.

"My dogs think beagle clubs are a vacation, and they act weird in them." I shrug, knowing full well that my dogs look like idiots as they run the paths.

It is a vacation from the hunt and a time to enjoy the hound music in abundance. I like beagle club breakfasts, and I like the sound of the wooden balls rolling out the packs. I am a Methodist, you understand, and never realized as a kid that the original purpose of those wooden balls was for bingo. I enjoy the philosophical debates on what makes a good beagle. I like watching dogs run— because although I do not attend many field trials, I want to know what bloodlines are available and where to get my future hunting dogs. I just might attend a few trials this summer. You might see me. I will be the guy watching my dogs run down a mowed path looking for a rabbit before I look at my feet and hope that if I am not looking at my dogs do this then you will not see it either.

BLACK POWDER BEES

My wife, Renee, periodically believes in things that make little or no sense to me. At one point, she was a big proponent of putting oregano oil on her face to stave off sinus infection. The net result was that she smelled like an Italian restaurant, and then she would go to the doctor for medicine a week later. She also had weird thoughts on honey, which she was sure would fix my seasonal allergies that began in August and extend until the first frost.

"The honey has pollen. It will fix you," she said.

"Is it weakened pollen, like a vaccine? How does it work?"

"Why do you have to know how it works?" she said, rolling her eyes.

The way it works is that it doesn't. Doing light exercise does help, however, as the breathing loosens up the congestion and allows me to hack, gag, wheeze, snort, and otherwise expel nasty things from my nose and lungs. So it was after drinking a cup of herbal tea sweetened with ineffective honey for the fifth consecutive morning without any benefit that I decided to go do some mowing on that August Saturday. I may have been a bit agitated since it was also the fifth consecutive morning without my standard caffeinated coffee. I lugged the lawn mower out of the garage and into the yard so that I could begin the process of starting the old mechanical contraption. Starting the lawn mower is a tricky process that is only slightly more complicated than the chicken dance. You have to pump the primer, pull the cord, and adjust the throttle in a series of apparently random sequences before flooding the mower completely. Then you need to cuss at the mower in a way that would make Yosemite Sam blush. Then you sit down and contemplate buying a goat to eat the grass. Lastly, you stand, pull the cord once, and mow.

I stood, pulled the cord, and then noticed about 1.5 million hornets buzzing around me, but not biting. I wondered where they may be coming from, and when I looked above my head, at the electrical meter head upon my house, I saw the biggest hive I have ever encountered. I thought to myself, "Wow, a nice hive!"

Actually, that was the second thought to enter my head. The first thought that I had was, "That is a massive hive that must have been growing all summer. I didn't notice it, but now I am really aware of the monstrosity that may, in fact, engulf my house. All of the commotion that accompanied the process of getting this mower started has really riled those stinging insects to life. They are blocking my entrance to the garage, and there is no way that I can get past them, so I better mow the yard, wait for them to settle down, and then return to the house, via the garage."

Those were my thoughts. And I did just that. Don't believe reports from my neighbors who claim that I yelled, "HOLY CRAP!" and pushed the roaring lawn mower in a zigzag formation through my yard. Renee has an account that may well agree, in part, with the neighbors' narrative. Her version differs insofar as she claims the word "CRAP" was never spoken, and instead maintains that I said another four letter word. My neighbors are not young, but I suspect their hearing is still keen, and we ought to put more stock in their version. I don't know how Renee could have heard me anyway, the mower was loud, and she was inside the house pointing at me and apparently laughing. At any rate, there is no reason that I could not have had the thoughts that I mentioned before while briskly mowing in the opposite direction of the hive. A zigzag pattern is not necessarily one inspired by an evasive technique, so much as a desire to manicure the lawn into hip patterns like professional gardeners might do. It is just harder to see the pattern in my complex mowing scheme.

Anyway, as I was mowing I began to think about that hive. It was huge, and I could use the hive for a lifetime of shot gunning! Let me explain. I came into the possession of a muzzle loading 16 gauge, percussion cap shotgun. It was made circa 1850 and is in fantastic condition. Beehive is a traditional material for the wadding. I received the muzzleloader from a relative that gets very involved with the period history scene. Authentic clothes, vintage accessories, and genuine passion for history are all part of the contemporary, muzzle-loader hunting tradition. He knows a guy that owns a pair of boots that were used in the filming of that movie called *The Patriot*.

"This is what you use as a wad to keep the pellets in the barrel," my nephew, Keith, said to me, handing me a zip-top bag filled with beehive."

"Oh," I grabbed the bag, "is that an authentic plastic bag holding the hive?" I joked.

"Of course not," Keith answered with a sincerity that implied my joke was not funny. "You would transfer some of the beehive material to your leather possible pouch when you go hunting."

"Okay," I replied.

"The beehive burns up when the gun is fired and mitigates against having a hole in your pattern as happens with a plastic wad," Keith looked at me over his glasses, the way I have been chastised by countless authorities over my life—teachers, librarians, doctors, and my wife.

Halfway through the zigzag-mowing session, the hornets appeared to be on the retreat. I began to think that perhaps I could get that beehive and have enough wadding to last quite a long while. I had taken the muzzleloader out last fall with limited success. I missed some grouse, killed some rabbits, and managed to limit on squirrels. One of the fun things about black powder is that you get to see all that smoke filling the air. I missed one squirrel, and although I can't prove it, I think I heard it cough before scampering up the tree to an upper limb and leaping to a neighboring tree to safety. It just didn't sound like a typical squirrel bark.

In my home state there is an early muzzleloader season for deer that allows for the use of percussion cap muzzleloaders. The traditional muzzleloader season, after Christmas, allows for only the more primitive flintlock guns. A 16 gauge is a .67 caliber, and a double barrel shotgun, although lacking the rifling, would still give me a second shogun. It would make for an ideal short-range gun in that early season—the second shot would be a great asset, I think, especially given the fact that my marksmanship with a muzzleloader could best be described as hit and miss. Mostly miss. I plan to try that this fall, as I have acquired some .67 caliber rounds.

So I tried to cut the nest down at night. It was really well attached to the house, so I found that in the end I had to make a retreat into the house. I waited until the next day and used a can of that long range bee spray, concentrating my aim on the entrance into the hive. They tried to escape, but many fell to the ground in their attempt. And then the can of spray ran dry. The can claims that it sprays twenty-seven feet. I ran very quickly, and the hornets closed the gap even quicker. I had been meaning to get more exercise, so I walked the four miles into town since I was blocked from the house by the swarm. Actually, I ran the first mile or so, as the hornets appeared to have quite a bit of animosity. I think I could have stopped running after the first quarter mile, but the combination of adrenaline and hornet poison propelled me an extra three-quarters of a mile with some degree of vigor. I wish I had a stop watch, as it was probably a better time for the mile than I ran when I was twenty and skinny.

I bought as much bee spray as I could buy with the money in my pockets. I had forgotten my wallet, but had a twenty dollar bill and some coins. So four cans of the brand that was on sale was my purchase. I had enough to get a can of soda pop, too, which was good after the hectic sprint. I plotted my strategy on the way home. Two cans into my assault upon the nest, the bottom third of the hive fell to the ground, exposing the interior and apparently killing the last of the bees. I saved the remaining two cans. A week later I harvested a bunch of shotgun wad from the side of my house.

The second two cans of spray came in handy, because when I was closing the garden for the year, an angry nest of yellow jackets managed to chase me into the house. They had bored a hole into the soil and had their home set up in a subterranean fortress. I couldn't have been stung more than a dozen times, at the most. My wife is concerned that our garden will not be organic next year, because I flooded the hole with two cans of bee spray. She was not interested in removing the yellow jackets, however, and she has plans for me to remove a few shovels of soil from the garden.

"Look at the plus side," she said. "Bee stings are outstanding for curing allergies."

I think that is untrue, as a score of stings in two weeks has not improved my stuffy nose in the slightest. But I plan on having a full day of busting bunnies with the muzzleloader this year. I wonder how those mountain men gathered beehives? They were probably smart enough to wait until winter, as they were wise enough to not own a lawn or a mower.

SOON

"Want to go on a romantic drive?" I asked Renee.

"Sure," she beamed. "Can we go see the sunset someplace on a hill?"

"Great idea!" I seconded her thoughts.

Soon we were on a dirt road. I was straddling the truck's differentials over some serious holes and ruts. My wife bounced around the cab. I mostly stayed still, my head only hitting the roof a half dozen times, because I had a steering wheel to hold as I drove. "Did you say romantic drive?" Renee asked as her butt lifted off the seat.

"Yep," I answered. "How do you like the view?"

"This looks like the kind of place that psychopaths take a woman to murder her," she said. "Or where a woman kills her husband for taking her!" Renee likes TV shows about crime. She even watches a few shows about women that kill their men. One is called *Snapped*. The other is called *Wives with Knives*. I reached into my truck's center console and moved the Swiss Army knife to the storage bin built into the driver's-side door.

"Oh, you will like the view up here, honey," I said with one eye on the road and one on her. "There is a handle there on your right side by the door. Hold onto it if you are sliding too much in your seat on this rough road." I figured it might be in my best interest to have her right hand occupied in the event that she wanted to be a wife with a knife and had her own hidden dagger somewhere.

"Are we there?" She held the handle with her right hand and the dashboard with her left.

"Very close. Just a few more switchbacks, and we will be."

"How many more cliffs?" she asked.

"Those aren't cliffs. Just washouts."

We rounded the last inclined curve and crested the top of the hill. There we were on top of an old mountain top that had been cut clear for timber. "Where are we?" my wife asked.

"A spot that had gypsy moth damage a few years ago. A logger told me that he was hired to clear cut this. It should be good rabbitat." Rabbitat, of course, is a term that means good habitat for rabbits. I slammed my truck door and walked around.

"Clear cut?" she yelled out the window at me. "You aren't trying to spend time with me! You're looking for rabbits, aren't you?"

"Sorta," I answered and spread a wool blanket on the hood of the truck and set up a little snack of sandwiches and freshly picked blackberries. My wife loves blackberries, and her eyes lit up. "But we are gonna watch the sunset. Then we will see how many rabbits are on this dirt road as we drive out."

"So you don't have beagles in the dog box?"

"Nah. You would have heard that. They go nuts the moment the front tires leave the hardtop," I said, "and go totally bonkers by the time the back wheels are on the dirt, too."

"Yeah, I guess you are right," she calmly spoke. "Hey, what are those sandwiches?"

"Smoked Salmon," I said, "like those ones we had on vacation that you liked."

"Really?" She smiled. "Where did you get them?"

"A bunch of guys from last year's fishing trip," I said. "We thawed them and Lenny had a new smoker he wanted to use. I even got some of that green stuff at Wegman's." Wegman's is a grocery store I rarely go into. It is for people who do not have jobs and like to spend an entire day navigating the aisles of a large food maze looking at things that are hard to pronounce. No doubt you have a similar place near you.

"Pesto!" she grinned.

"Yep," I said. "Green stuff."

We watched the sun sink into the Laurel Highlands before driving home. "Look at that!" I yelled as several rabbits frolicked on the dirt road in front of us, dusting themselves before running into the thick underbrush. We rounded another curve, and there were two more rabbits that streaked into the living walls of thorny, green vegetation. "I have no idea where I will get a shot at these rabbits other than this road, but man there are rabbits here."

"Yeah. Just let me know how that works out. You might be making me car sick," Renee said.

"You sure it ain't bad fish?" I asked. "There was some debate about the appropriate temperature for making smoked salmon versus salmon jerky."

"No," she leaned over against me, "it is definitely your driving."

"Sorry. If I don't do this, we will get stuck in those ruts,"

"Those are ruts?" She strained to see the sides of the road. "I thought they were gullies."

"I might come back here in the morning to see how the rabbit chases are," my voice quivered with excitement. "I can leave here another way and make a meeting in the other direction after the chase."

"Oh, great," she said. "A longcut." Longcuts are what my wife calls my shortcuts. She says this because they often do not save as much time as they do miles.

"C'mon," I pleaded. "This would be a shortcut. Not a longcut."

"Yeah," she snickered. "I will get a phone call at quarter after nine saying that you are late for a meeting and they want to know if I reminded you."

"That is rare!" I stuck my head out the window to ensure I had enough clearance. "At least in recent years," I clarified.

"It isn't a shortcut if it is twenty-two miles of road that is a dotted line on a map with no cell phone reception," she howled.

"What are you talking about?" I disagreed. "I think the dictionary lists twenty-two miles of unimproved road as the very definition of a shortcut. I got those blackberries you ate tonight from a bush on that road you are referencing. It was just last month. It is very accessible when it hasn't rained recently."

"I still say you were on a blackberry expedition, not a shortcut," she mumbled under her breath.

By the time we got back on the hardtop road, I had counted a couple dozen rabbits. I probably counted more deer. The night drive is a good way to get a preliminary census. I knew I would return with a dog that was deer resistant. When I was younger I would use the term deer proof, but I have since stopped using that language. That was because I found that my old beagle, Lady Day, was no longer deer proof. She wouldn't start a deer chase, but if some other dog did start a deer run, she would gladly take the front and show you how it was done.

In the coming days I investigated several other similar locations. Talking with loggers is a key part of my rabbit hunting success. It is a good way to find new spots. I have also moved a few pairs of brush pants and a wool shirt into my truck. My rubber boots—standard for summer when my sorties afield with beagles are confined to morning chases on dawn dew—are now joined by lightweight, leather boots as well. The September air is cooling, and evening rabbit chases are about to replace the early morning ones.

I was in my study, just yesterday, taking an inventory of shells. I use a .410 when the briars are thick and the shots are all close. I prefer a 16 gauge for the more open shots after the brush is battered by the frost. I even take a 12 gauge on rare occasions when I think I will find pheasant. I was making a mental note of what shells I needed to buy when my wife walked in. "It looks like rabbit season is here," she said. "The backseat of your truck is full, and you are cleaning a shotgun."

"Not yet," I said, "but soon. You want to go for a ride with me tomorrow night? I got a hot tip on some rabbitat."

"You have any more blackberries and salmon?"

"I have frozen blueberries and trout," I said. "You bake a pie, and I will take a grill for the brook trout and cook them for you. What do you say?"

"Sure. I like to have an idea where to send people to look for you when you break down in the middle of nowhere and don't have a cell phone signal. You have to be missing forty-eight hours before I can report you as a missing person."

"What?" I asked. "How do you know that?"

"I like to know your hunting spots, so if I don't hear from you, I can send your friends."

"You don't tell my friends where I hunt do you?"

"No," she said. "But if you get stuck or broke down, I might have to send them. I think forty-eight hours would be a long time to have to wait before calling the police."

"I will go thaw the berries and trout." I walked past my wife, making sure she didn't have a knife in her hand before turning my back.

BEAGLE FEVER

Amazon, as you no doubt know, has changed the way that we shop. I somewhat like the ease of getting stuff without having to go anywhere. No doubt it is bad for small businesses, but if you live in rural areas, there aren't many of those—but I do go to the small stores for as many things as I can. I have to drive forty minutes to find any bookstore, let alone a non-chain store. For those of us in country places—and many who own beagles live in the boonies—it is not easy to find a store that sells the stuff we want. Brush pants, briar-proof shirts, and even pocketknives are hard to come by in most stores. I can wait two days and have the things I order online. What is the appeal of such a fast delivery to me?

When I was a kid we would drive to a Sears store. I ain't talking about a store that you walk in and see all the tools in one area and the clothes in another, then all the household goods over in some spacious corner. Our Sears store was smaller than a seasonal ice cream stand. You walked in, and there were three or four appliances for sale. They took up most of the floor space. There was a counter where you could place an order. One employee was all that was needed. You ordered from the Sears Catalog. For the youngsters, this was a catalog that came to the house periodically. It was the size of a large city's phonebook, and dropping it on your foot would not be recommended. When you went to the store, they had the same catalog, and they would order the item you wanted. It was a half-hour drive to the Sears store. There was no way of knowing when your ordered item would arrive. A wait of a week or more was not uncommon. The store would call on the phone when the purchased item arrived. If you were ordering something you needed for Christmas or a birthday you made sure to allow several weeks for delivery, just to make sure.

When I first got beagles as a kid I would order things from the various outdoor catalogs—Bill Boatman, Nite Lite, Cabela's, and others. They still had COD then, or cash on delivery. You could call a company, and they would send you the stuff you wanted, and for an extra fee you could pay the delivery man cash when it got there. No credit card or bank account needed. Can you imagine the wad of cash that the UPS man had to be carrying in those days? Anyway, this COD option was great for a thirteen-year-old kid with no checking account—but it required that somebody be home when the delivery was made.

No problem. My mother, seemingly, was always home. She cooked, cleaned, and did all the things that make a family get along. Years later, after my sister and I were raised, she took a job outside the house and found the minimum wage to be a great increase in her wages (she worked at home for free) and she also found that the workload was lighter and only a mere eight hours (a full sixteen hours less than the days she worked when raising kids). I was gainfully employed as a paperboy and had money to waste! Oh, for the youngsters again, it used to be that kids were paid to deliver newspapers. Newspapers, by the way, used to be the way that most people got their news. There were no twenty-four hour news channels to speculate on a missing Malaysian airplane for twenty-three of those hours, even if all the known information concerning said airplane could be read in a mere two minutes. Newspapers still exist, but their future seems uncertain. Oh, and they are always delivered by a retired man who drives a car with a loud muffler. Unlike the loud cars young people drive, the paper man's muffler is not intentionally loud, it is falling apart. He throws the paper in the general vicinity of your house as he drives by. Our paper has three puzzles—the crossword, the jumble, and the hardest of all—finding the damn paper in your yard.

Anyway, I delivered papers. Oh, and I delivered them to the customer's house, I might add, often placed between the storm door and the main door of the house. This kept the paper dry and out of the weather. Some houses preferred the paper on the porch, but it was heavy enough not to blow away in the wind. Modern newspapers are smaller than the inserted advertisements that went inside the newspapers of old! My mother could have worked in sales for a Fortune 500 corporation. She could talk a hungry dog off a soup bone. She made sure that I was always getting new customers for the paper. I won a trip to Europe the first year I had that paper route. The *Erie Sunday Times* newspaper sent two kids on the trip, which was sponsored by *Parade Magazine*. They sent an "Erie kid" and a "country kid" as they called those of us who lived in the rural places. I inherited the paper with customers numbering in the low 30s. Mom tripled the number of subscribers, and for each new customer my name went into a lottery. I won, but only because all Mom's friends started getting the paper! I saw Italy and what was then called Yugoslavia. Not long after returning from Europe I bought my first beagle, which I found in an advertisement in the *Erie Sunday Times*, and I paid $75 with money made from the Sunday paper route. It was a lot of money when I made 15 cents per delivered paper. It was all those new customers that Mom got for me, and kept getting, that allowed me to fully fund my own hound dog enterprise. Dad bought a beagle as well, so we had two.

I was hooked on a lifestyle with these beagles. I bought coats, hats, belts, belt buckles, and stickers—all depicting beagles. All of them delivered COD. My mom was also my banker for the paper route. My pockets were crammed with coins and paper money, and I dumped it all on the kitchen table upon returning. Mom would count it and put it in the zippered bank bag. The comics and inserts for the newspaper arrived on Wednesday afternoon. The representative for the newspaper would bring them and collect the money I owed him. Mom took care of that, as I was rarely home on Wednesday afternoons—I was in the woods with my beagles. The news portions of the paper landed with a thud on my porch sometime between 3:00 a.m. and 4:00 a.m. on Sunday morning. I woke upon hearing the noise (as did the rest of the house) and assembled them for delivery. In time, my family learned to mostly ignore the thunderous noise of all those papers landing on the porch. They must have been thrown from the driveway, which was ten feet or so from the house.

Fancy stainless steel water and food bowls were bought with that paper money. I also bought leather leashes and a wallet that had an image of a running beagle burned into the leather. I had a plastic coin purse with a beagle on it, and I kept it packed with quarters when I collected the paper money after the *Erie Sunday Times* jumped from sixty-five cents to seventy-five cents, though most customers gave me a dollar and told me to keep the change.

I would call the toll free number in the catalogs and get gear using the cash on delivery payment option. Mom would get the money out of my bank bag when the package arrived. She also sewed beagle patches on coats and searched my pants pockets for shotgun shells before doing laundry.

Mom saw that I had the beagle fever. I could walk to an area and let my dogs chase rabbits on a neighbor's farm. Unbeknownst to me at the time, she would walk up to the farmhouse and visit with the neighbors long enough to verify that I was indeed in the woods with the dogs.

"Why did you do that?" I asked her when I was in seminary and pastoring a church.

"Just to make sure you didn't lie to me and go into town and get in trouble. Your father and I never cared if you went to the woods, it was the activity in town that scared us."

"How did you know that I didn't leave the dogs there to chase and then go into town?" I raised an eyebrow to make her worry.

"HA, HA, HA!" She slapped the table. "You would have never left those dogs out in the field without you. If you had your way, those mutts would have been in the house. That is also why I drove your dad to work on Saturdays after you turned sixteen and got your driver's license—so you could run dogs!"

"Oh, c'mon, you did that 'cause I begged Dad for the truck." I pushed my hands towards her as if to give her argument back to her.

"Well, you weren't exactly easy on that old pickup, and it cost more to maintain when you bounced your way into hunting spots." She gave her argument back. "But I told your dad that if you were allowed to go rabbit hunting on Saturdays you would not stay out too late or get into too much trouble on Fridays."

I was thinking about all of these things about Mom while at the bank not long ago. I occasionally go to book signings and sell copies of my books. I was stuffing the money into a little box and transporting it to the bank in a plastic bag to make deposits. The bank teller said, "I'm tired of you bringing in that money in a sandwich bag!" and handed me a vinyl bank bag with a zipper, one that looked much like the one that my mother used to keep my paper route money in, with the exception of the fact that it had a different bank logo on it.

"Thanks," I said, looking at the bag. All those memories of the paper route and the beagle pups, and all the COD deliveries hit me at once. Heh, I probably made more money pedaling newspapers than I do at most book signings, but I still use the money for beagle stuff. COD is a thing of the past, so I have to take the money to the bank and deposit it, but that free, two-day delivery gets things like stickers and hats and coats to the house pretty quick!

Looking back at all my mom did for my beagle fever, I have to be thankful. Hound music has been good to me, and the only way to get a kid interested in hunting with beagles is to have parents that encourage the outdoor lifestyle. Just looking at the zippered bag makes me think of walking in the pre-dawn hours to deliver those papers, counting down the weeks until I could afford my own beagle. Yep, my mom knew that I had the beagle fever for life. And if she was alive today, she would not be surprised that I have moved the mutts into the house with me.

"Hello?" the bank teller said.

"Pardon?" I answered

"You zoned out on me there, where did you go?"

"Oh, I was just thinking of something," I said, looking at the zippered bag. I thanked her and walked outside the bank, thankful for the beagle fever and more thankful for the woman that encouraged it. Happy Mother's Day!

JANUARY

Okay, I will let my southern friends in on a secret. If you listen to us northerners talk, you might be convinced that it takes a special subspecies of beagle to chase rabbits on snow. The term "snow hound" is thrown around with reckless abandon, as if this were some breed other than a beagle. Well, the truth of the matter is that snow is more difficult scenting than other conditions. However, a hot, dry August day is also poor scenting conditions. In my experience, the hounds that do well in one also do well in the other. Myths, of course, abound.

I hunted swamp rabbits in Alabama with some guys that read one of my articles and invited me down to hunt. I stayed in a hotel so as to not impose, and if I ever get the opportunity to go back, I will stay in their homes, as we quickly went from strangers to good friends. One morning, while drinking coffee in a Bama motel, the guys called me and said, "Hey, we aren't going out till 9:00 a.m. because of the frost." They, of course, didn't see many frosts, and the hounds did not encounter them enough to actually get accustomed to it. But they had some GOOD hounds that did very well on other poor scenting conditions. Frost, like snow, is another variety of tough scent. I really think that good hounds learn to adapt, and they learn to differentiate one type of bad scent from another. I have owned good dogs that look bad on the first snow of each year, the same way that they look bad on the first dewless morning of the summer. It is the same with how they look bad for the first hour on the first frost, or the first trip into the old coal strip mines that have more dirt and shale than grass. Poor scent makes good dogs adapt.

All of which is not to say that there aren't some hounds that are better on snow than others. My old Rebel is the best snow dog I ever owned, and while his strong nose is a contributing factor, he also hunts with his eyes. He has learned to identify what rabbit tracks look like, and he scans the snow for the telltale ovals. Of course, he uses his eyes when snow is absent as well and looks for small tunnels and game trails burrowing through the underbrush. Rest assured, a good dog is a good dog—period.

Even so, there is something about winter that gets me excited to hunt bunnies. All of those days afield in November that yielded great chases and few shots become more fruitful. Where the standing goldenrod allowed the rabbits to run past me, sounding like a freight train but remaining invisible, the very presence of a few inches of snow provides a back drop of white that makes a brown cottontail stick out like a sore thumb. They are not camouflaged in the slightest. I sometimes feel a little sorry for the little lagomorphs, the same way that I feel sorry for stark white snowshoe hare as they sit motionless on barren ground, convinced they are invisible when the snow has either not yet arrived, or fallen and melted.

Here in Pennsylvania we have a very short season for hare and a daily limit of one. So I go to the Adirondacks, my wife's home, and hunt them when we go to see her family at Christmas. You are allowed six hare per day, and I have gone there for a week and returned with as many as thirty-four. Old Rebel looks for their tracks, and if the ground is hard and frozen, temperatures at zero, he adapts by the second day, chasing the big, white critters the same as he does a brown cottontail on an August afternoon, slow but sure across the terrain. I still find hare to be the most magical of all rabbit hunting, as the rabbits are not easily seen. Once the bunny is started, I find a spot and wait as the dog circles the hare. I stand with my eyes intentionally unfocused, standing statue still, looking for moving snow in my blurry peripheral vision. I then shoot the "moving snow," which is the hare. A few times the only way I found the dead hare was by seeing the drops of red blood that fell out of the nose to mark the powdery white snow. Winter hunting makes hunting grounds a few miles from home seem like a wilderness. Deer season is over, and all of the guys that claim to be hunters, but only hunt deer in the rifles season, are out of the woods. I like the cold wind, and a successful season finds me with scarred lips, chapped by the cold winter wind.

As I prepare for the second rabbit season, which runs from the day after Christmas until the end of February, I am bombarded by hunting catalogs. New technology oozes through every page, with promises to ward off subzero temperatures and moisture. When it comes to winter, I do not think we have really improved on clothing since God made sheep. Wool is warm, keeps rain and snow out, and allows sweat to escape. While it is prone to attracting burdock, it does not make a "swish" sound with every step. It isn't too bad at repelling briars either. The drawback of wool is that it is scratchy to some people, especially my wife. She won't come near the stuff. But hey, hugs and kisses aren't the reason I go hunting anyway!

Lately I have been hunting Rebel's pups, now three years old. They are good dogs, but not as good as their father. I feel like those long-tenured football coaches who start kids for no other reason than the fact the kids had fathers that played on his team in years gone by. Sure, the dogs are good, but not (yet, I hope) as good as their progenitor, who was able to circle rabbits time and time again, his powerful nose bringing the bunnies back until I got a shot; but the youngsters do shine, and I hope they will improve, especially as the snows stack up and the powder renews itself, adding an inch or two every other night.

On a calm day, with little wind, the January sun shines as the temperatures hover in the twenties, or less. The baying of the hounds seems infinitely crisper as it echoes off the hills, and the sound of their voices carries just a little further than it did in November. The tone seems brighter and clearer, too, and I love to be out there in the woods, no one else around. Most sportsmen are inside, preparing for spring turkey season, or even cleaning favorite reels in anticipation of the first day of trout fishing. Maybe a few are out on the lakes, ice fishing for a fresh meal. I continue at my usual pace, each day producing a couple hours of hound music and a rabbit or two as well. As the snow relentlessly pounds the fragile vegetation, the bunnies tend to concentrate in the thicker areas by the end of January. Some days are characterized by long chases, with no shots, as the bunnies stay to the interior of dense patches of greenbrier or multi-floral rose. I abandon my 16 gauge shotgun for the ultra-light .410 and enjoy the music —no sense in carrying a heavier gun when I might not get a shot! Even so, I do get a couple more cottontails in the game vest.

Few things make me as happy as walking out of a secluded, snow-drifted valley, wearing snowshoes, the weight of a couple bunnies pulling on my vest in the back, and a few beagles pulling on leashes in front of me. And while it is small game hunting—not an exotic hunt for Caribou in Alaska, or Moose in Canada—it is still hunting. And the noble rabbit is pursued by every critter that eats meat. Coyote, fox, hawks, owls, bobcat, weasel, and even crows are probably better at killing bunnies than me (hey, crows are murder on a nest of baby rabbits in the spring). And for this reason I find the rabbit to be worthy of admiration. We do not have to spend a bunch of money to chase them, and we do not have to pay a guide to locate them. In some ways I think they are the best indicator of a healthy habitat and sound ecosystem. Now, if you will excuse me, my wife wants to go to the movie theater and said she won't put her head on my shoulder if I am wearing this wool shirt. Hmmm, maybe I will get more popcorn if I leave it on?

FEAST

It seems to me that people routinely take occasions to overeat. When I was in college we would go to a place after our softball league played that sold 10 cent wings. Or, and many did this, you could get all you could eat for five bucks. I wasn't a math major, but that meant you must eat at least fifty-one wings in order to save any money, which we did. Granted, we were poor college kids and would skip food all day, leaving us hungry by the time the game ended at dark, but that is a lot of calories in one sitting. All you can eat buffets seem to offer the same sort of easy access to gluttony on a daily basis.

I am over forty now, and I try to be good about what I eat. What I mean by that is I confine myself to things that don't have much taste as much as possible. I eat more varieties of lettuce than I can name. A dozen wings would be tough for me to finish. At twenty-one I could eat a couple score of wings and go back out to play another game of ball. I had a metabolism that allowed me to do stuff like that. Nowadays, I have to admit that 220 pounds was a powerful body in my prime, but would be a doughy one now. My arms have shrunk. My stomach has enlarged to compensate, however, so I stay balanced. At one time I could haul 200 pounds of dog food at one time—a bag on each shoulder and one in each hand. Two bags are sufficient for me now, though I will kick it up to three bags to try and impress my wife, but she seems not to notice.

Thanksgiving, however, is a day when all bets are off, and the entirety of the hunting season prior to the holiday is devoted to this feast. Now, I should explain that we only have wild game at our little feast. Furthermore, we only invite people that appreciate a meal comprised of meat that may contain the sporadic shotgun pellet. I was once told that people in the Mediterranean expect to find pits in their olives, because that is just natural. That is how we feel about the occasional peppercorn that turns out to be lead shot. You spit it out like a bone and move on with the meal. It is not noteworthy. When I was a kid the Thanksgiving feast always involved turmoil. There were several contributing factors to this overall chaos. One was my grandmother's insistence that we have a capon in addition to the turkey. I have often wondered what poor guy had the job of turning a rooster into a capon, but given her gruff disposition towards most men, I think she preferred to think of herself as psychologically emasculating most males. Finding a capon isn't the easiest thing to do, and only a few stores sold the damn things. If Mom was on top of things, she would buy one any time after September and freeze it until the day before the holiday, and then tell her mother that it was fresh bought. If she failed to do this, then Wednesday of the holiday week was pretty much a disaster as a neutered rooster was hunted down like public enemy number one. One year we considered taking an axe to a rooster twice— once on the neck and once a little lower to create a post-mortem capon. Gram was pretty serious about this holiday requirement.

On one particular Thanksgiving week I hunted a farm that belonged to some family friends, and I had a heavy game bag as I returned to Dad's truck at dark on the day before Thanksgiving.

"I heard some shooting, how did you do?" Claude said, forking some hay in the barn.

"Great!" I beamed, "Four bunnies, a grouse, two squirrels, and a bunch of apples off that old tree at the corner of Sam's pen. Sam was the bull, and he owned the farm. Even today I could dive safely between two strands of barbed wire if I had to do so. The trick is to cover your eyes as you lay yourself out like a base stealer on a head-first slide. Sure, the wire gouges the forearms, but that is a far cry better than horns gouging the backside.

"Those are sour apples." Claude heaved a final bit of hay and put the pitchfork in the corner.

"Yeah, but Gram likes that kind for pie and strudel."

"Oh yeah, those would be good for that. Haven't had strudel in ages." The farmer scratched his belly.

"I will bring ya some," I said, the dogs tugging at the leashes.

"Ooh, thanks. You cooking any of that game tomorrow?"

"Nah, they already thawed some rabbit from the freezer."

"How's your folks?" Claude was now grabbing a can of fuel to fill his tractor.

"Miserable. They are out searching for a capon for Gram. You know how she gets. The stores all sold out or didn't get any. Mom was on the phone making phone calls all day to butchers."

"Shoot, I got one here. Probably not as fat as those store bought ones. There are five left in that pen coop behind the laying hens. Ain't no need for more than one rooster. They don't fight once you turn 'em into capons. Go get one."

"Say, Claude, that sure must take a sharp knife, eh?" I asked.

"Just go get the damn thing," he chuckled as he reached on the wall for an axe.

The only one happier than Gram when I returned was Dad. "Thank God," he said, "I am going to get a nap before I go to work tonight." He wasn't really going to sleep; he was just hiding in his bedroom and reading newspapers and magazines. Gram had that effect on him. Gram was excited because the capon was missing his head and entrails, but all the feathers were still there. She loved plucking chickens. She ran out in the yard with a tub of hot water and soaked the bird and plucked. She then came inside and grabbed a thick wad of papers off the counter to burn the fine, hair-like remnants of the feathers off the skin. I looked out the window and saw a blazing conflagration as she held burning papers in her hand, the flames licking all around the poultry, her face being the only thing visible in the night.

Dad walked downstairs. "Hey, did my *Sporting News* come yet?" That was a paper that he got in the mail. Mostly he liked it for baseball, and in the fall and winter he liked to keep track of all the trades and free agencies."

"I put it on the counter." Mom's voice was muffled as she slid another round of pies into the oven.

"What the hell is that!" Dad looked out the window, amazed at the fiery sight before him. "Some kind of pagan ritual?"

"Nope," I said, looking at Gram. She obviously held the burning paper too long and burned her hand. "That is *The Sporting News.*"

"I'm going back to bed," he sighed and walked away, obviously angry about the paper.

"I have to get a brine for this thing to soak overnight," Gram said as she walked in the house with a slightly blackened bird. "This is going to be perfect."

"I think I will turn in for the night," I said, grabbing a hunting magazine and meandering upstairs.

"Send your sister down here to help!" Mom yelled. Sis was hiding in her room, too. Dad taught us well how to deal with Gram.

Thanksgiving Day always had me hunting, because there was a cornucopia of conflict as Mom and Gram tried to make sure that all the food finished cooking at the same time. I would go to the woods and return after noon. The feast was always between two and four, but there was no real way to predict the exact time. The essential thing was to be hovering nearby, because when the table was ready, we were all forced to eat "while the food was still hot." I have never understood the appeal of shoving steaming forkfuls of a meal into the mouth, but this seems to be important.

I guess that is the stuff that makes the holidays special. It is the weird stuff that makes sense only to the family that is directly involved. Like my own little wild-game Thanksgiving. There are a few things always on the menu —rabbit for one. Squirrel potpie is another. We always have garlic and lemon stuffed trout, cooked on the grill. Stuffed pheasant and grouse are favorite treats as well. Woodcock is almost always one of the dishes consumed first—beagles flush a lot of woodcock in some of my favorite bunny spots. If I get a deer in the archery season, we have venison tenderloin. If archery does not go well, I will be out hunting deer on the following Monday—the gun season always opens the Monday after Thanksgiving.

On years I shoot a fall turkey, we pound the breast and bread it to be cooked like chicken fingers. Fruit pies are everywhere, depending upon what I was able to scavenge that year while running dogs. Blackberries, blueberries, and strawberries are often mixed into the same pie. Apple strudel is a staple, and, for the sake of tradition, we have a pumpkin pie. There is always sassafras tea from roots I picked, and we have no set time for anything. We just cook stuff, and as it is finished, we eat—that would drive my gram and my mother crazy. The day progresses as a series of samplings. All my hunting buddies can stop by whenever they like, and people tend to come and go throughout the afternoon. More than a few people have gotten in trouble for eating light fare at their own family dinner and then filling up on my famous rabbit stew or rabbit fajitas. There is no formal seating, and people can eat wherever they like. Throwing chunks of fat, scraps of meat, or trout skin to a beagle is encouraged. Taking a nap on a couch or easy chair in between samplings is a big part of the day. At least one pie will be left too close to the edge of the counter and will be consumed in a skirmish of tri-colored hounds while we are snoozing in the living room.

Last year my mother-in-law was still living with us, and she and my wife had several disagreements about the meal before the big day even arrived. I knew I had better hunt for the morning, my father having taught me that two women cannot cook in one kitchen. "Be like seeing a ship with two captains," the WWII Sea Bee said. So I went afield and enjoyed the morning. Well, I hope you enjoy your Thanksgiving. I will even share my favorite rabbit recipes with you. You can find them at www.beaglebard.com. The only ingredient not listed in those recipes is the sporadic peppering of lead shot—that is dependent on your own shooting skills.

INVASION

Invasions are odd insofar as some are welcome. Napoleon was not greeted with love by most of Europe, but there were Greeks in modern Turkey that celebrated the arrival of Alexander the Great. No doubt you can think of other examples. In the hunting world we often hear the term invasive species. Often it is not a term of endearment. Talk to the avid trout fishermen in the Rocky Mountains, and you will find that the brook trout is viewed with almost the same disdain as people have for the Asian carp in the Great Lakes. Brook trout outbreed the native rainbow trout and cause problems for the native trout to thrive in their historic ranges.

Africanized killer bees make the news. Nobody wants them. Feral hogs are so common that they are devastating large chunks of land in many states. They are the wild descendants of the pigs that pirates and explorers left on American soil to ensure readily available food when they would return to a certain area at a later date. Nutria are rodents that were raised for fur but some escaped, and now the big semi-aquatic critters are causing trouble as they are native to South America, and they have thrived in the States, displacing other animals and destroying the environment. They over browse the fragile marsh vegetation and leave the soil prone to erosion.

But there are invasions that no one seems to care about. When is the last time you heard, "I wish that the damn brown trout was never brought here from Europe!" or "They should have left the pheasant in Asia where it belongs!" I have never heard a deer hunter unhappy about apple trees, which are not native to this continent.

Apple trees in the woods are some of the most sought out locations for archery hunters and rabbit hunters alike. It isn't at all unusual for my beagles to have a very productive day in the vicinity of small, wild apple groves. A full game vest has bunnies, the occasional grouse, and enough apples for a pie. On days when the rabbits are not presenting themselves for a shot, a good day hunting simply means tired hounds—and enough apples for two pies.

As a beagler and a rabbit hunter, I am also pleased about a few invasive species. One is the European hare. I would love the chance to hunt one of these. They were raised on farms in earlier times, and some escaped—like the nutria. New York State once had a bunch. Southern Ontario still has a sizeable population in places. What a thrill that would be to go to Ontario and hunt the hare that our beagle ancestors were bred to hunt in Europe. It would save a lot of money on airfare to Europe to hunt them. I would view a hunt like that with the same enthusiasm that a big game hunter would have when approaching the opportunity to go after an Alaskan moose.

"Why are you smiling?" my wife said to me the other day. "You are bleeding!"

"The dogs ran out of hearing today while they were chasing a rabbit. I ran over the hill to find them, and they were in a spot I have never been—the biggest patch of multi-floral rose I ever saw. It was beautiful ..." My wife shook her head and walked away, mumbling something about strait jackets and rubber rooms. Multi-floral rose is an invasive species, although it was intentionally planted in this country before anyone figured out that it would be as prolific as it was. Rabbit hunters are probably the only people who like seeing this stuff. It provides year-round cover for rabbits, which is welcome to me, especially since many of the mountain tops that were strip mined for coal are no longer capable of growing anything but grasses, and they disappear in the winter. Multi-floral rose was once planted as a living fence to contain livestock and as a crop that helped prevent soil erosion. Then they figured out that the birds poop the seeds, and they land on the ground in nutrient-rich bird guano, ready to germinate.

I feel affection for autumn olive as well. It provides great cover for rabbits, and it is spread by bird poop, too. I belong to a beagle club that is packed full of this stuff. We always have plenty of rabbits to chase. I understand that autumn olive and multi-floral rose both tend to force out indigenous shrubs as they spread, but I am also never disappointed at seeing either plant when I am afield with the hounds.

Burdock was brought here by Europeans. It may have simply clung to someone's clothes and been deposited upon arrival, but I think kids probably brought them. We had burdock battles all the time when I was a youngster. The stuff was impossible to get out of your hair, and I think that is how the "bowl" haircut originated—when moms had to shorten their daughters' hair after a burdock battle. My first flat-top haircut came after a prolonged burdock battle that raged for days when we found a bunch of it growing on a vacant lot.

When the frost knocks down the goldenrod and the snows bury the grasses, I still find rabbits in thick clumps of burdock. I think I may be the primary distributor of this invasive species. I pull the sticky seeds off my hunting clothes all the time and just drop them. The beagles carry the seeds as well. If the grass gets away from me in the lawn, I can see young burdock sprouting. No doubt the dogs deposited these seeds there the previous fall. During the hunting season a burdock burr will get lodged into the couch blankets by a beagle, which causes much marital stress as my wife pulls a fleece cover up to her neck on a cold evening and finds that a scratchy burdock now rests upon her arm.

There is a bird hunting club not far from me, and some of their game birds make their way onto public land. It was the first time I ever saw a Chukar. No one ever complains about these birds being invasive any more than they do the pheasant. They are a tasty bird. We catch brown trout, eat pheasant, and chase bunnies through autumn olive and multi-floral rose. At the end of a hunt I pick burdock seeds off myself and the beagles. All of this involves invasive species. I have to reconsider how I feel about these invasions. It is the kind of thinking best done over an apple pie.

TROPHIES

Whenever I see the hunting channels on television it seems somewhat disappointing to me. Maybe even a lot disappointing. It has to do with the animals, to be honest. The trophy mentality has taken over. The television shows are all about the kill and watching the impact of the bullet or arrow, and then assessment of the dead critter based upon its measurements. Bears have their weight and height taken. Deer must have their antlers tabulated into a raw number that quantifies the overall value of the animal. I was watching one such show where the guys were in palatial tree stands and trying to determine which monster buck to shoot. Large deer were all around them.

"Here we are in the wilds of Pennsylvania," the guy said, "and we are surrounded by trophy whitetail."

I have lived almost my entire life in the Keystone State and have never seen that many large buck at one time. At the end of the show they gave the name of the guide. A quick Internet search showed that the place was remarkably close to me, and it may as well be categorized as a deer farm. They feed and raise the deer in a giant pen. After you shoot your deer, they determine how much money you owe based upon the size of the animal— thousands of dollars being a likely fee.

Those of us who hunt with dogs are the folks I think could be a corrective to this mindset. Oh, before I go on, I should say that I am not opposed to labeling some animals as trophies, and I am not opposed to spending money at the taxidermist. It is just that it seems wrong to reduce hunting to a review of the newest equipment and a mathematical description of the prey's vitals after it is shot inside of a fence. Hunting is about the story for me—the day, the people we are with, the dogs that accompany us. Killing animals is a big part of what we do, but it isn't that big of a deal—and I confess to having taken a few of those pictures with the beagles on the tailgate surrounded by bunches of bunnies.

If we forget that hunting is about introducing youngsters to the sport and making sure that Grandpa gets to shoot rabbits without having to chase after the dogs, then we have missed out on a big part of why we hunt. When we narrate the chases and the shots and the kills but neglect the skill of the hounds and all that they do even when we miss or do not see the rabbit, then we have misplaced our focus. It seems somewhat anticlimactic to describe a chase based upon the data recorded by the tracking collars on our beagles:

"How was your hunt?"

"Good. Dogs went 14.4 miles and averaged 4 miles per hour."

None of that seems to put the proper emphasis on the chase, the scenting conditions, the fact that the old veteran hound kept the chase going across a two hundred foot stretch of solid rock, or the times that the rabbit doubled back on his tracks to try and escape. These things really do matter. What is a trophy rabbit? I have only paid taxidermists twice in my life—once for a varying hare because they are not common here, and once for a swamp rabbit since they only exist in certain parts of the South. If I hunt other species of rabbits not found here, I will probably pay for a taxidermist again. I have some antlers in my house, but nothing I ever paid a taxidermist to mount.

I have, at times, been unable to shoot a rabbit that has given a particularly good chase. I can't explain it. And I am not overly proud of the fact. I can simply say that my goals on any hunt are: 1. Safe dogs 2. A good chase 3. Dead rabbits. When a rabbit runs far and wide and then stands stark still in front of me, I sometimes find that this wonderful creature has impressed me with its tricks, sprints, and tenacity. Sometimes I let it go past me. This is as close as a hunter can come to catch and release. I almost always shoot the running rabbit. It isn't until it stops and looks at me that I appreciate all that it has done to live this long despite the fact that everything wants to eat it. Hey, before I wax poetic too long, I must admit that I often blast the little guy right where it pauses, especially early in the season when the freezer has no rabbits!

Maybe that is a big part of this discussion—the fact that the trophy aspect of hunting ignores the reality that we have just killed supper. I know people who kill deer and give the meat away. I am not sure why they hunt. My wife was cleaning the closet when she stumbled upon my deer trophies—spikes and Y bucks, a few six points, and a couple larger sets of antlers. Most of them were fork four points. Did you notice that I quantified the animals there?

The bigger four point was my first deer, and I can still remember how excited I was and that my dad was even more excited. There was a spike I shot when my dad was dying of cancer and not working—we really did need the meat. The big seven point was my first archery deer, and it walked right up to me dumb as a switch during the rut. I could give you more details on all of those deer and the other antlers. Likewise, I can narrate the wondrous aspects of rabbit hunts. I can explain the joy of being shown a great spot by a retired hunter who swore me to secrecy. Haven't we all experienced that superb run at last light when the scenting conditions drastically improve as the warm ground meets suddenly chilling air? Can't we describe that strong-nosed dog that barks and babbles on morning dew and frustrates us by not producing a rabbit only to impress us in the afternoon when the sun dries up the scent, and her strong nose is what makes the chase possible?

All of this and more is what makes hunting the great sport that it is. Next month the season opens for many readers, and we will be storytellers. I am sure that I will tell that story with a Facebook post of dead rabbits more than once, but I sincerely hope that I will also tell that story in terms of the intangibles, the things that can be qualified but not quantified, and the way that hound music shakes our soul. In many ways our trophies are the pedigrees of our hounds and the memories of days afield. I hope to hear your hunting stories this season.

HUNTER'S FEAST

Halloween is the most dangerous of all holidays at my house. The reason is because my hunting hounds live in the house and chocolate is poisonous to pooches. Our kid routinely left his candy sitting where it was easily found by dogs. We had a few incidents where we called the vet at night due to a discovery that the dogs ate an unknown quantity of chocolate. She told us to get a turkey baster and force feed hydrogen peroxide to the hounds every ten minutes until the guilty glutton regurgitated all the chocolate and wrappers. It takes two adults and a child to force feed the liquid to a twenty-pound beagle, for the record. We gave each beagle a dose, which took a little over ten minutes, and then repeated the process until the desired results. You haven't lived until you have had four beagles in various stages of canine-vomit convulsions on your kitchen floor.

Anyway, our child is now too old for trick or treating, so we just sit home and wait for the kids to come get candy now. But kids eat candy all the time nowadays, and so they feel no need to gather it in season, like early man must have done with berries or other fruit. I had a ton of leftover candy this year—miniature Milky Ways, Snickers, and Three Musketeers. I felt the only safe place to stow these delicacies was in my truck console, which is where they have been since November 1.

I will munch a few as I drive to a hunting spot, and a couple more on the way home. The only ones I really like are the Snickers, but I unwrap them without looking (hey, my eyes are on the road) and wait to see what I randomly chose. Statistically, every third candy bar is a Snickers, and therefore a happy event. Well, actually, it is probably a higher rate than that, as I gave out mostly Milky Way bars until I realized that all three bags were not the same. My wife quickly poured all the candy bars into one big bowl and gave the costumed kiddos their choice. The candy is about gone now, and hopefully I walked enough during the hunts to burn the calories. The hunting trips have been fruitful, with lots of small game in the freezer—which got me thinking about freezers full of meat.

When I was single I held the alternative Thanksgiving. It was for hunters. I devoted the entire month of November to this meal, hunting all sorts of game species. I always had rabbits, squirrels, pheasant, grouse, and woodcock. Beagles flush a lot of birds while chasing rabbits. Many years I also got a turkey. When I was willing to leave the hounds at home and grab the bow, there was also venison for the big meal. I used the charcoal grill outside for a few thawed fish from the summer—native trout and maybe some catfish if I had them. Basically, the success of my November determined the menu and the number of guests that I could invite. I made a lot of things that could be prepared in slow cookers, such as squirrel pot pie, grouse noodle soup, and venison on weck, so that I could also hunt Thanksgiving morning (you can do a google search for a beef on weck recipe and substitute venison if that regional term is not part of your local landscape). All of those dishes were bubbling in the crock pots while I was in the field. After the hunt I would cook bird—wild turkey breast was sliced, breaded, and cooked like chicken tenders. Pheasant was stuffed with rice, wrapped in bacon, and oven roasted. Woodcock breasts were flash fried with onion and hot peppers, almost like a stir fry.

Guys would wander in and out of my house from midafternoon until well after dark, sneaking away from their own in-laws for a visit to my house. I had sassafras tea perking all day and added new water to the cut roots (I dug them myself) as it was consumed. A good sized root could flavor a lot of water, and I kept adding new root as the day progressed. Since I was a bachelor, it did not matter if people sat at the kitchen or in the living room. I allowed guys to wander wherever they might feel comfortable. We told hunting stories as we grazed on the smorgasbord of wild game. No doubt a few of the stories were true. Many of the men brought their sons to the meal. We always made a big fuss about their hunting stories, and a grey squirrel shot at twenty-five yards was given the same honor as a trophy buck killed with a recurve at forty yards. There was always much talk about the impending rifle season for deer, which always begins the Monday after Thanksgiving in Pennsylvania.

Beagles napped throughout the house, but they tended to curl up into pathetic balls at the feet of the guests, begging for a morsel or two of food. Their sappy eyes and thumping tails are very persuasive, and they did manage to get an occasional snack. Such panhandling was permitted on this holiday, as they were responsible for producing most of the meat that graced the table. Hunting topics such as shotgun gauges, shot size, and favorite knife brands dominated the conversations (16 gauge, #6, and *Case* are my preferences, if you were curious). Some of the guests were old timers that lived alone, but others were fellows who had eaten an earlier meal with family, but saved room for the alternative feast at my place.

And then I got married. I had my own family feast to occupy my day. Sure, I still got to hunt in the morning, but there was no meal with the guys. People talked about those feasts as if they were great events of yore! My wife overheard such a conversation recently, and had a great idea the next morning over breakfast. "You should have your Alternative Thanksgiving again this year," she said.

"What was that?" I feigned difficulty hearing her, as I raised an eyebrow to surmise if she was sincere, or just testing me.

"Your wild game dinner." She spread her arms across the table where she sat. "I think you should do it again. I will help. Did you ever have dessert at your older feasts?"

"No. I can't bake."

"Well, I can cook all the same wild game recipes that you can, and I can also add sides and desserts. That way you can invite a few more of the guys this year. And you can just have people come and go like you always did."

"Really?" I asked, excited about the last days before the holiday, eager to chase a few more birds and bunnies.

"Yep," she stood and rubbed my back affectionately before refilling her coffee, "and since I will cook, you can hunt a little longer on Thanksgiving than you usually do."

"THANKS!" I was ecstatic.

"It is the least I can do." She smiled. "By the way, my family is coming here to eat this year."

BEHOLD, THE RABBIT

Well, small game hunting is still in season, and we can get out there and bust some bunnies. To be honest, I'm glad that the fevered rush of deer season is over. Many of the "hunters" that I know actually just go out to chase deer for the two weeks that we are allowed to hunt them with a rifle. Don't get me wrong, I feel affinity with all hunters, but the crazed dash for antlers sometimes just makes me feel like not hunting. I try to get my deer meat in archery season, before rabbit season opens, in order to avoid the entire two weeks of rifled mayhem altogether. There is something about the sound of a half-dozen high-powered rifles rapid firing on a running deer a few hundred yards away that just makes me cringe.

Actually, I spend much of deer season walking around looking for rabbit tracks in the snow. I came home one day this year in cold weather just grinning. "Did you get a deer?" my wife asked.

"Nope," I said, giving her a hug.

"Why are you so happy then?" She pushed her palms against my chest, ending the hug.

"I found a ton of rabbit tracks!" I said.

"Any deer?"

"Sure, there are always some deer tracks, but there were lots of bunny tracks in there."

"Did you see any deer?" she yelled. "It isn't rabbit season."

"Sure. I saw deer. But man did I see rabbits. I can't wait for bunny season to come back in!"

Ah, but rabbit season is now in full swing again, and I am enjoying the fields and woods. I prefer running in the open and the wild areas. I haven't been to a beagle club to run dogs since the end of October, and I belong to two of them! There is something about the abandoned strip mines and the farmer's hedgerows and the national forest that make my hounds look better than they are. The rabbits do not double back on their own trail so much, and there are no mowed feed strips for the rabbits to run. In Pennsylvania many of the clubs were formerly operated by traditional brace enthusiasts. The result is that there can be parts of the club that have more mowed paths than brush. I understand that, too, as a couple rabbits running down a mowed feed strip may be enough to run first series for the brace guys. Repeat the same path runners after lunch, and the winner can be declared. There are no mowed feed strips in hunting season.

I also like hunting season for the fact that there is no fence. Don't get me wrong, I like having a fence at the beagle club when I am conditioning dogs, but it is sometimes a false sense of security. Fences get holes, and sometimes they get knocked down. It is roads, not fences, which I worry about in gunning season. The one thing I do miss about the club running grounds as the season rolls on to the end is the abundance of rabbits. In fact, it is for this reason that I simply do not shoot near as many rabbits as I once did. I still get over fifty in any given year, but I no longer feel a need to try and eat every rabbit the dogs chase. In fact, I have gotten to the point where I am not shooting rabbits. The old timers warned me about this. They said killing critters would get problematic for anyone that loved the hunt.

It is the chase that has caused me to pass up shots. If a running rabbit sees me and stops, it is safe. I see the twitching ear and the great, big eyes, and I just can't shoot. I know it is unaware that I can kill from a distance, and it pauses hoping I do not see it. If I take a step in the rabbit's direction, it will bolt. If I wait a few more seconds, the hounds will be close enough to get the bunny hopping again. Sure enough the rabbit runs, but having seen it motionless, I often cannot bring myself to squeeze the trigger. If the rabbit is a good runner and stays above ground, I am especially unwilling to shoot. I want to make sure I can come back and get good chases

I don't want to sound too sentimental. I still do shoot many, and I can't explain the full reason that I kill some and let others pass. I am definitely happy with just one rabbit on any given day. I think I admire how the bunny has managed to survive so well, despite the fact that everything wants to eat him. Did you know that a cottontail can run almost 20 mph? A snowshoe hare can get closer to 30 mph. Jackrabbits can get going closer to 45 mph. When you account for the small size of a rabbit, you are talking about a critter that if human sized would be running about 120 mph. We have all heard that speed kills, but in the case of our favorite game animal, speed is what saves it.

Oh, they have a flexible joint in their skulls that functions as a shock absorber and allows them to see well even with the jarring that pounds their skeletons at top speed. Speaking of sight, they can see nearly 360 degrees. Ever been on a small hill and mounted your shotgun as a rabbit passed below, only to have it change directions suddenly? They can see above themselves, too. That comes in handy when all those critters with wings are trying to have you for a meal.

Sometimes, after a deep snow, I am amazed to see the bark chewed off trees at the height of my chest or more. The adaptable rabbit gets by when the snows cover the more succulent vegetation by eating whatever can be reached. I am shocked to see how small they can make their bodies. I have watched full-grown rabbits squeeze through a single diamond of chain-link fence. I have also marveled at how high they can jump and watched my old Rebel tree a rabbit once. Well, it may have been six feet off the ground, but still ...

Any beagle club will talk of the predators that threaten the rabbit population. Hawks and owls are perpetual aerial threats. Crows can wipe out a nest of babies. A weasel problem is a near disaster. Fox and coyote are expert rabbit hunters. A feral housecat can do heavy damage to the rabbit population, so imagine how many the bobcats eat. Talk to our northern beaglers, and they say that a single fisher can put a dent in the club's rabbit count.

But here is what amazes me. You can hunt a spot with dogs and never turn up a single chase—even with the best jump dog you ever owned. Then you go back there in the summer, and the bunnies are there in such numbers that you have no trouble getting your pack of beagles thoroughly tired on great chases. Some years there are more than others, but the resilient bunny always comes back. I can conclude a hunting season at the end of February with little or no chases, and by June I'm at my wit's end trying to keep them out of the garden.

My backyard is fenced, and the bunnies are foolish if they sneak in there, because that is where the beagles roam. My front yard is not fenced, and that is also where the dryer vents. Oftentimes, in February, there is exposed lawn there from the clothes dryer melting the snow. I can see rabbit tracks roam over there to look for the yellowish blades of grass. I put bruised apples there. I also put the last few baby carrots that get slimy in the bag there. I like to think that it helps the rabbits through the winter. I have a few hunting spots within a mile of my house, and maybe overpopulation in town helps the numbers where I actually hunt.

Anyway, like I said, I am not sure why I shoot some rabbits and do not shoot others, other than I want to get good chases. When I was a kid I thought any day that did not yield a limit for the freezer was a bad hunt. The older hunters warned me that the day would come when I would change my mind about these things. And sure enough it did. That being said, I have recently killed a rabbit that was giving me great anxiety. The dogs had run him more than a few times this year. I thought he was evading my dogs by going underground, because the chase always ended in the same spot. But I realized it was running along the edge of a steep bank of shale (left over from a strip mine) to get away. I figured this out because one of the dogs managed to wind enough scent to lead the others along that steep wall of rock. It was steep enough that I worried about a dog going over it and getting hurt. So I stood there whenever a chase went into that area. The rabbit kept going in another direction, but I refused to move, because I was afraid a dog might get hurt. I finally got the dare-devil bunny, as it was hopping straight at me along the wall; and I have to say, it felt pretty good. Those of us that are beagling enthusiasts know the joys of rabbit hunting. The hunting programs on television seem to think

that all the fun consists in waiting for a buck to walk
under a baited archery stand. I still say nothing compares
to the excitement of a pack of dogs in full cry. Someday I
am going to write a poem. It will be an ode. I will call it
"Behold the Rabbit."

KITCHEN TABLE

January brings kitchen tables to my mind. Kitchen tables are amongst the most important places in a person's life, or at least they used to be. It is common now for people to meet in restaurants or coffee shops, but kitchen tables are more appropriate. My childhood home had a linoleum floor, and in the winter it was over half covered with little throw rugs. The throw rugs rested under the chairs so that people could sit while wearing their boots, the melting snow seeping into the fabric of the rugs. People would pop in and out of the house during deer season or a day of hunting small game. There was always cold tea, hot coffee, and a little snack.

The table doubled as a map. Stories were told by moving cups, paper towel rolls, salt and pepper shakers, and other assorted items to represent known physical landmarks so as to explain where a certain event happened. In the first week of January this map was used to detail the location of varying hare in the Allegheny National Forest. It was a short hunting season for the white ghosts, and the daily limit was just two. Today the limit is one. They were found in the big woods, at higher elevation, and we often needed to wear snow shoes to plow into the towering hemlocks to chase them. This was before GPS and training collars. The elusive bunnies were always found where the deer population was more plentiful than any kind of rabbit. The baying of the hounds on a hare sounds pretty much like a trash run on deer—big circles large enough in diameter that you could not hear the dogs any longer. If you had a dog that was prone to deer, it was worrisome to go out there. I always got ready to shoot when I could hear the dogs' voices starting to return. It wasn't unusual to shoot one several hundred yards in front of the dogs, especially if the snow was deep and the dogs were slowed.

At that time, most of the beaglers I knew ran traditional brace dogs, and there were not many of us hunting rabbits at all, let alone going deep into the national forest. The devoted hunters met in kitchens, and topics of conversation in January were often about hunting. We also talked about things now seen as antiques—studded tires and snow chains. Another popular debate was various ways to safely add weight to the bed of a truck in order to improve traction. We used bags of sand. We naturally were always looking for farmers with straw, which was our preferred bedding both for the kennel in the yard and the crates in the truck.

It was also at the kitchen table where I learned to cook. By learn to cook, I mean I watched my mother cook. I never cooked a thing, actually. Surprisingly, this taught me a lot. Granted, I can't bake, but I am able to whip up some vittles that taste good. When I was a single man I went through a phase where I refused to buy meat, opting to live on wild game alone. Naturally, I ate domesticated meat in restaurants and at other people's homes, but I only ate wild game at home. The idea to live this way hit me as I was mad at some cows. I was hunting at a farm, with just one dog, Rebel, and he started a rabbit in the goldenrod. The chase quickly entered the cow pasture where it ended, right alongside the barn. I then noticed my dog running for his life as the cows tried to stomp him to death! I ran towards the beagle and started whistling loudly with my fingers. Rebel ran towards me, thankfully, and we moved towards a new patch of brush. He bounced another rabbit out of some greenbrier, and the result was the same— Rebel running towards me after the chase ended at the barn. I later learned that the rabbits on that farm all tended to run under the barn and stay there. My dog had a little limp, and I wondered if he was cow kicked. I got up close to the pasture and had disdain for the massive beef cattle. They walked at me, happy to see a person. I then had a thought, "Why would I eat anything too stupid to know that it is food?"

So I went wild, or at least I ate wild. Squirrels, rabbit, grouse, venison, and pheasant became the meat in my house. Sure, deer provide a lot of meat, and a fellow could get a buck and a doe. But it seemed I ate a lot of rabbit. I mean, the merry beagle helps us out by chasing the rabbit until we get a shot that we can make!

I remembered all the recipes that Mom made, and I altered them a little, in small ways. The alterations were not entirely intentional; in part they were because I could not remember everything that she did. Mom didn't write down her recipes, and when she died they died with her. I, for one, find that writing detailed recipes is not all that helpful. We all have different tastes. For instance, the only difference between Sloppy Joes and my wife's chili is that she puts kidney beans in it. Before any Texans write me, I know that beans are supposed to be off limits for chili! I keep a super-hot salsa in the refrigerator (Mrs. Renfro's Scary Hot Ghost Pepper Salsa, made in Texas) and put a few spoonfuls in my bowl to add the heat that I like. Or sometimes I put my wife's chili on a hamburger bun and pretend that it is a festive Sloppy Joe. The festivity comes later, compliments of the beans.

I do not remember the television being on much until after supper when I was a kid, so we never gathered in the living room. Homework was done at the kitchen table. Minor repairs were done there, too, rather than going to the workshop in the basement. Eye glasses, various toys, and small appliances all got their maintenance on that table. That is also where kids sat to have tiny splinters of wood and thorns removed by Mom and her sewing needle and tweezers, as the brightest lights in the whole house were in that room. Daydreams were publicly spoken there, some that came true. I filled out my college application on the kitchen table (after it had been cleaned with a dish rag and dried with a towel) and became the first in my family to go to a four-year college. The table was also a place where contingency plans were formulated to address life's uncertainties. Bad news goes down better with banana bread or cake.

I miss the importance of the kitchen table. Families don't even eat there together as much as they once did—kids have so many evening sporting events, dance recitals, karate lessons, and scout meetings. Where an evening away from home one night each week was then a rare treat, now it seems that an evening with no scheduled activities is the elusive joy today. As a pastor, however, I get to see the kitchen tables of people's lives more than most. I hear the great joys of lives and pray with people during tragedies. The mail sits on the corner. A pen or two is always nearby. I think the table could become sacred space again.

Sure, I know that the past is gone, but if I could bring back one thing, it would be the kitchen table. I like getting directions with cups and sugar bowls as landmarks. Most of my friends now e-mail GPS coordinates to me, and I would gladly trade the precision of those numbers for the certainty conveyed in the spoken word. I am looking for the journey that leads to the destination. The soul of the table seems ripped out of it when the parents eat there while the kids eat in front of various electronic screens. Heck, I was in a restaurant for lunch the other day while returning from hospital visits and a mom and her child were watching a cartoon together on a smart phone while they ate. Even tragedy seems to have left the table in favor of Facebook, where mourning is done publicly. There is something about regular old coffee—Maxwell House, Folgers, or some other easily found brand—served in a ceramic cup with a small chip in the brim or handle, that makes the fancy coffee shops seem artificial, or worse. Pie should be served as a slab that covers a small saucer plate, whipped cream slapped on top of it, and yet the gathering places today will serve a sliver, with the whipped cream placed around the edge of the plate as decoration.

My friend Lenny was in my kitchen the other day. He grabbed his favorite coffee mug from the cupboard, filled it to the brim, and then grabbed a few cookies, which he placed on a paper towel. "I found some snowshoe hare!" he gasped. "I was out bear hunting with some guys last month, and I thought I saw one jump out in front of me. Well, I went back, and I confirmed it!"

"Really?" I slid my chair closer to the table. "Where?"

"Okay," he said, wiping the table to test it for cleanliness before sliding his cookies off the paper towel in order to use them as points of familiarity on the kitchen table map. "Here is the place we were that day that we both shot grouse," he said, plopping a cookie down. "Up here is that spot where you got your truck stuck last winter." Another cookie landed.

"Wait," I interrupted, those spots are miles apart. Where is the river bottom where we had to drag that big deer that was so heavy when we were kids?"

"Well ..." He scratched his chin, holding a quarter that was sitting on the table in the air as he mentally calculated the spot, and then put it down with a confident slap. "About here," he said. "And the hare are between there and the spot where we drug that deer. Off of that old clay road."

I grinned, knowing exactly where he meant. "Hey, we can get in there pretty easy," I said.

We made plans, dreamed of big chases, and cleared the map when my wife returned with a bag of groceries. We might even shoot a few white ghosts there. My favorite way to eat hare is in chili, using a recipe my mother made, mixing the meat with a little venison. I have other rabbit recipes as well, all kitchen-table certified. You can adjust them anyway you like. Shoot, you can even make the chili taste like a Sloppy Joe if you want.

SWAMPY

We are into the heart of summer, and while many people are happy to lounge in the heat, it is a hazard for training dogs. Of course, I still think that for many people the outdoors is an alien place they only endure briefly in between the car and the next building. This reality has even infected my own home. This is the first year that my stepson has really mowed the lawn. In years past, my wife was overprotective and felt that he was too young to handle the job without hurting himself.

"I think he can handle it, hon," I said, when the topic came up last winter. Wesley was shoveling snow for one of the first times in his life, and the topic of lawn care ensued.

"But," she brushed the hair out of her eyes as she loaded a full magazine of worry into her mouth, "there is the road that you have to walk near and the blades are sharp and he is clumsy. I just want to make sure he is old enough to do it."

"Am I big enough?" I asked.

"Yes."

"Well, I am six feet tall. And your kid is taller than me. I started mowing the lawn when I had to reach upwards to grab the handle."

"But look at him!" she yelled. Wes was flinging shovels of snow over his shoulder, launching it high into the air, much of it landing on his shaggy hair.

"Ah, no problem," I said. "The lawn mower stays on the ground."

He has done well with the grass this summer, although early in June he worried me when he came inside to ask a question. "Bob," he spoke in his surly teenager monotone, "I just have the side yard left to mow, but came in to see if I had enough daylight."

I was speechless. I stared at him in disbelief. "Well, do I?" he grunted.

"Sooooo," I said, "you were outside, where the sun is, and you came inside to see how much daylight is left?"

"Right. So, do I have time?" he cleared his throat while speaking the words.

"Yeah," I tried to exude the patience that one might need when explaining something very complicated. "You have a couple hours. I am just now getting ready to take the beagles to the woods." He went back outside to finish the lawn. I was horrified that a person would not know when it got dark, or that looking at the sun was not even remotely helpful in helping a person determine this basic knowledge.

It gets worse. The daycare sent out information to our friends about International Mud Day. Apparently mud is such an alien concept to kids that they celebrate a day at the end of June when they intentionally get the kids outside and let them play in the dirt. The parents have to sign a waiver permitting this day in the mud. It is like they are allowing the kids to do something typically off limits— like staying awake until midnight on New Year's Eve. The kid can stay awake late once per year and play in the dirt once per year. People walk around with antibacterial gels and wipes at the ready as they program entire days for their children—indoors.

July is very hot, and as a kid I used to take my beagles to a swampy area to let them chase bunnies in the early morning or late evening. The swamp was within walking distance of home, and it required rubber boots even in the hottest part of summer. It was the kind of place where you could find skunk cabbage and soft clumps of grass that you could hop-scotch to stay out of the black mud. The grassy clumps mostly kept you from sinking knee deep into the soft bottom land, although there was always a few that looked large and sturdy but were not weight bearing. In other words, I went home muddy every day.

Returning home from a morning afield required me to pass through security before being admitted into the home. Boots were left outside after being hosed off with a garden hose. I then had to stand in the laundry room and strip down to my underwear before going directly to the bathroom in order to remove all the mud from my body. My mother preferred that I weed the garden after exercising the hounds and before returning to the house. Too often I would bathe, put on clean clothes, and then weed the garden, hence requiring another bath. Even worse, I might make a second trip to the swamp in order to run the dogs again before returning home after dark. I was fourteen years old and lived outside for the summer.

The swamp did have copperhead snakes, but I had never seen a snake bite a dog before and didn't worry much about it. My dad always said that you could smell cucumbers in the air when the copperheads were around. I once smelled a copperhead in the swamp, but never did see it. This could be due to the fact that I set a new land speed record on my way out of the muck and onto the dirt road where I could see what was around me.

My wife, I have determined, does not do laundry nearly as often as my mother did. She always makes sure that I have clean slacks and clergy shirts for work, but Renee is decidedly indifferent towards brush pants and blue jeans. She tends to wash her own clothes and Wesley's with a lot more frequency.

"Have you seen any of my brush pants?" is a common question that I might ask.

"I think I saw them in the dirty laundry pile," is her common response.

"Oh. All of them?" I scratch my head in disbelief.

"Yep. I started doing laundry when I was so young that I hardly had to bend over to get it out of the basket. I'm sure you're old enough to do laundry if Wes is old enough to mow."

I still tend to spend time in the swamps during the hottest months. Insects give me more worry than anything, between the mosquitoes carrying West Nile disease and the ticks carrying Lyme. I like to train the hounds in places where their bellies stay soaked and they have plenty of water to drink. Granted, I carry water to the woods with me, but I have found no way to prevent a beagle from drinking out of the nastiest mud puddles.

The fascinating thing about the morning sorties into the swamp is that the dogs are mostly clean by the time they get home. They dry off in the dog crate as the wind generated by the drive home passes over them, and they are merely dusty when we return. This dust seems almost invisible until the hound runs, jumps, wags its tail, or barks. At that point, you can see tiny clouds puff into the air. Renee then gets out the vacuum cleaner to chase after the dust bunnies. Or dusty beagles. After one trip to the swamp, she seems to have had enough stress from the dust.

"SEND ONE OF THE DOGS UP HERE!" she shouted from upstairs.

I walked over to the stairwell and looked up to see my wife standing in a one-piece, blue bathing suit. The beagle enthusiastically followed her into the bathroom, and I heard a series of yelps, howls, barks, and bawls. The beagle made some noise, too. There were the tell-tale sounds of splashing water and the thump of beagle against the porcelain tub. Soon the beast was in full retreat, storming down the stairs and doing barrel rolls on the floor in front of me trying to get the clean odors removed.

"NEXT!" she stood at the top of the steps, hands on her hips, like a gladiator determined to destroy all challengers. The next dog was not willing to go upstairs. When he got up there he made a sound that made me wonder if he was being water boarded. Two more muddy pooches were waiting for their turn. They tried hiding, but Renee went on the offensive, slowly stepping down the stairs and strutting the way a professional athlete might make a dramatic entrance onto the field in an attempt to intimidate the opposition. She took them both upstairs at once. They too ran downstairs when their baths were over, tails tucked low as they dried themselves by rolling on the couch.

I decided to go look at the bathroom. I'm not a forensic specialist, but I would classify the room as displaying signs of a struggle. In our bathtub/shower there is a bottle of shampoo and a bar of soap. Oh, and there are approximately forty-nine other things that I can't identify—various conditioners and lotions and oils and exfoliates and scented things. Typically those items are precariously balanced along every flat surface inside the tub and on the shower walls; and they are so densely packed that you cannot move the shower curtain without tumbling a dozen of these containers into the tub like dominoes. All of these items were floating in an inch of filthy water along the tub floor. Mud and silt lined the sides of the tub. The shower curtain was rent open and appeared to have sustained permanent damage. Renee sat on the side of the tub, water dripping from her entire body.

"Now what?" she said in an eerily calm voice, the opposite of her shouts earlier, and yet somehow more intimidating. "What do you have to say?"

"Nothing." I slowly turned towards the door. "I just came up to tell you that I was going to do some laundry."

Stay cool in this heat, my friends.

BORED

In Pennsylvania, Father's Day and the end of the school year can be close to the same day. It all depends on the weather. Schools often plan for snow days, but in the event of a hard winter we often find the school year extending into the first weeks in June. When I was a kid this meant that I had to mow grass when school was still was in session. Furthermore, I had to cut grass in a part of the world where nothing was flat. What I mean by that is that yards were too hilly to push a mower. Houses were built on a flat pad that was bulldozed into the earth, while the rest of the yard was on a virtual mountain. Families would routinely hire boys to mow these steep yards. This was done by tying a rope to the mower and lowering it (attached to a one hundred foot rope, often a clothesline) to the bottom and then raising it again by hauling it hand over hand to the top, before lowering it again to the bottom in order to repeat the process. This seemed normal as far as making money for the summer was concerned.

My stepson, apparently, is much smarter. He simply says, "I am sad" or "I am bored," and people throw money at him and volunteer to take him to toy stores and places that sell video games. When I was a kid I once said "I am bored," and I was sent to the yard in order to make sure that there was no chance that the lawn could come near the backyard sidewalk, as I was ordered to the task of jabbing a flat hoe alongside the cement walkways in order to prevent any vegetation from contemplating the possibility of growing near the cement walks. Years later I saw a power tool on wheels designed to do the same task. Children were born, in my family, to do the labor that expensive tools could perform. Boredom was viewed with the same disdain as communism or atheism. For the most part we finished morning chores and vanished into the summer air, as simply sitting still and catching your breath could be interpreted as boredom.

Since school always lasted until the first week of June in northern Pennsylvania, I would spend those days staring out the windows of the classroom, watching the trees bloom before my very eyes. Any amount of snow during the winter months meant that school could last a few days longer, or even a week. My friend Stump owned his own truck (a gift from his dad) and would drive me to school on any given day after his sixteenth birthday. I was forbidden from riding with him, as we were always late for class. Most kids found a car to be a most desired alternative to walking to the school, but Stump seemed to view his wheels not so much as a ticket to liberation, but rather as a new means of lethargy. He would sit in his house until the last possible second before we raced into the truck like the start of the Le Man race and then speed up the hill to school. We were perpetually one minute late. His homeroom teacher seemed to see a minute of tardiness as no more than a minor inconvenience. My homeroom teacher, by contrast, saw the same minute of delay as more of a capital crime, routinely proposing that I be executed from the nearest tree by hanging. Teachers are always warning us about our "permanent record," and my parents were certain that these tardy statistics would prevent me from getting into college, finding a job, or getting married.

As a result, I was forbidden from riding with my friend to school, at least after the first report card demonstrated those tardy statistics, and I had to walk. I was then early, opting to do homework in my seat rather than socialize before class. This protocol of early arrival conditioned me to a new reality: if I was "on time," no teacher thought much about my presence for the remainder of the day. I could be on time for the first bell, when attendance was taken, and then disappear. I often found my escape during the time period between the first and second academic classes of the day. I would sneak out the back door, into the woods, and then rush home towards my hounds. I judiciously scattered these days throughout the year in order to coincide with small game season, trout fishing, and the training of beagles.

Naturally, I didn't skip every day. I planned my excursions around test schedules and found that with careful deliberation I could miss most of a school day without any single teacher wondering about my whereabouts. The irony, of course, was that my family forbade me from riding in a vehicle that got me to school one minute late, when walking resulted in my arriving early and skipping most of the school day on certain occasions.

June, arguably, was the most difficult time to remain inside. I found the entire premise of spending all day inside a building offensive, and it seemed odd to me that we were cautioned to study hard so that we could get an "office job." In my experience, an office is as much like a prison as it is a place of work. Looking out the window makes me wonder about the wind and the sun, the feel of the air, and the temperature conditions.

On one June day of my junior year I was hard at the business of skipping school while listening to the beagles chase, when I heard my father's voice behind me, "Shouldn't you be in school?"

I turned around quickly and didn't even offer an excuse. Dad sat on the log next to me. I was wearing my school clothes, and I noticed that he was wearing a polo-style shirt with three buttons and a raised collar. Those were not his work clothes. "You and Mom were both gone so I grabbed the dogs," I confessed while never making eye contact with him.

"I know." He put his hand on my shoulder. "I kept waiting to see the dogs come out of their box and onto their wire runs in this warm weather, and then I went outside to notice they were missing. I figured you must have been involved and couldn't have gone too far without the truck. This spot seemed like the best place to look for you."

"Why are you wearing that shirt?" I asked. "Did you go to the school?"

"No," he said in a deep voice, drawing out the "o" sound to indicate that I had no reason to worry.

"Oh," I said, "that's a relief. I don't have any tests today or anything."

"I had a doctor's appointment today," he explained his shirt. It was the first of a series of such appointments over the next two years, as his cancer was no longer in remission, though no one knew that at the time. They thought his pain was caused by any number of other factors.

"Feeling okay?" I asked.

"Yeah," he said, my back hurts a lot of days." We sat on the log and listened to the chase.

Months later, when school had resumed after the summer break, Dad approached me one night and said, "I have another doctor's appointment tomorrow. In case you want to meet me at that log with a rabbit chase later in the morning."

And so began my parentally sanctioned truancy. Over the course of many months they determined that the cancer had returned. Each doctor's appointment was a day that required my missing school so that we could talk about the big things in life, not the least of which was death, all while the dogs sang their song of pursuit. I still process the big things in life with the benefit of hound music. I write sermons, funerals, and even magazine columns while listening to dogs—a notebook and pen are always with me. As Father's Day fast approaches, I find that some people are too overcome with the grief of having lost their own father to enjoy the day. Oh, this is a tragedy. Even if our fathers have passed away, we can still cherish the good memories. Sure, the last couple years of my dad's life were painful and filled with trips to the oncologist, but if I dust off those most recent memories, I find that the tears give way to laughter and all of the great things that can be shared between a father and a kid.

Father's Day is a chance to remember all the good times. All living dads can share the good memories with us, but even if our father has passed on, we can be filled with thanks rather than sorrow. And if you see me staring out a window on a sunny day, I am not bored. I am still afraid to say that word for fear of having to edge a sidewalk. I am merely plotting an escape from the office.

LAST BIT OF SUMMER

It seems hard to believe, but school will be starting again very soon. As I remember things, I was always disappointed to be returning to school at the end of summer break. It was hard for me to transition from the nearly three months of being outside to having to go indoors for the duration of the school day. I ran my beagles every day of summer vacation when I was a kid, even if it was for a short duration because of heat. I picked berries, shot groundhogs, cut grass, and caught fish for spending money. Things were different then. At that time, parents avoided their kids by having them do chores whenever they were caught at home. The result was that kids would leave the house as early as possible so as to not have extra chores heaped upon them. When I say early, I mean 6:00 a.m. sometimes. I would leave a note saying that I took the dogs to the woods. My mom would find the note when she woke up, or sometimes Dad would find the note when he got home from work. Our parents' sanity depended on our leaving the house.

In fact, I am convinced that the volume of commercials on television promoting medicine for mental disorders is primarily caused by parents spending too much time around their kids, who never leave the house without adult supervision. Parents are forced to transport youngsters everywhere, and then wait for them to finish playing with a friend before driving them back home. I am not even sure that kids have a bicycle nowadays. The bicycle was our primary transportation. Oh, and not only were we not required to wear a helmet while riding, we were actually punished if we wrecked the bicycle and got hurt.

"What's that bruise on your arm?" a dad would interrogate.

"I wrecked my bicycle," a kid might panic and be honest.

"What? Did you scratch the paint? What did I tell you about that? If that thing rusts out or gets broken, you are not getting a new one. Maybe you better run alongside your friends as they ride their bikes for a few days as a punishment. That way you might learn to respect your things and not ruin them. You can have your bicycle back in a week."

Notice how there was no concern for the bruise? The kid should have lied, said that he got beat up by another child when asked about the bruise. He may have gotten yelled at for fighting, but at least he would still have his bike. Our parents always presumed that we were at fault, unless there was overwhelming evidence to the contrary.

Parents avoid their kids nowadays by putting video games in their bedrooms and letting them sleep all day. I once walked into my stepson's bedroom, and the hum of electric devices and the dim light inside made me think that maybe I was in a nuclear submarine. It was mostly video games and music-playing devices, with the computer screen devoted to a video chat with friends. Apparently the kids will text each other on a cell phone rather than make a phone call, because holding a phone to their ear is too restrictive. Yet, they will sit at a computer for hours, their butts glued to the seats, and stare into a video screen while they are having a conversation.

Fishing was my favorite way to make money. Jay and Maize was an older couple that lived nearby, and they always gave me $.50 for a trout. They really liked trout, and Jay wasn't able to fish as he did when he was younger. Spring-fed creeks in the area had active trout even in the hottest days of the summer. I am sure I made more money cutting grass, but it was a lot more fun to catch trout while my dogs were singing a rabbit chase.

Anyway, the month of August was always a sad one for me, as I dreaded the daily companionship with beagles and fishing coming to an end. I would take my two beagles to the creek every day and let them chase rabbits until they were panting heavily in the summer heat. Then I would tie them to a tree in the shade while I fished for fifty cent pieces, also known as native brook trout. I also had another spot that I liked to take the dogs where there were not trout but carp. A big carp paid a dollar from an Italian lady that barely spoke English. She wouldn't buy a small one. No one where I lived ever ate a carp, and it wasn't until I was an adult that I learned many Europeans consider them a delicacy. Regardless of whether I fished for trout or carp, I always took the hounds and let them chase until they were tired. I don't recall ever seeing a deer tick in those days, and I would often lay in the shade with the beagles after they drank water from wherever I was fishing. I kept fish on a stringer in the water so that they did not spoil. I had learned that if I delivered the fish to my customers in the late morning, I was often offered a Popsicle in addition to my pay. The Italian lady always had banana Popsicles, which were my favorites. Jay had the more traditional flavors.

I did not have a fishing vest at the time, and I carried everything in a tackle box, including the telescopic fishing rod and reel. If we believe the outdoor catalogs, we might think that catching native trout entails big sweeping casts over our heads with a state-of–the-art fly rod as we stand in chest-deep water looking for rapids, pools, and eddies to cast a perfect fly into the spots that hold ravenous fish. The reality is that I crawled as quietly as I could on my belly, tied live bait onto my telescopic rod, and let it drift downstream. The creek (pronounced crick here) was narrow enough to step across in many places. The canopy of underbrush and trees was so thick that attempting to cast could have resulted in catastrophic results, the most pleasant of which was sinking a hook into your own skin, the worst of which might lead to breaking a rod. The worst part of crawling towards the bank of the stream was anxiety about rattlesnakes. Sometimes a beagle would be in the brush as well, moving sticks and twigs as it looked for a rabbit. When you are on your belly, all noises sound like a warning from a timber rattler.

Crayfish tails were my favorite bait for native brook trout. Crayfish could be found in great abundance by turning a few rocks over in any river and catching them. I would rip off the tails and put them in a small container that sat in my tackle box. Worms were harder to come by in the dry times. The trick was to use a small bit of the meat so as to not allow the brook trout to steal the bait—a couple crayfish would last all morning. I normally fished for carp with leftover crayfish that had been "aged" to the proper scent. Aging crayfish is easy—you just leave it sit in the tackle box on a hot August night, and in the morning you have aged bait.

The beagles, naturally, would try to get the fish. I had to make sure that the stringer wasn't in water where it could be accessed easily by the beagles. I learned this the hard way when I was trying to figure out what animal ate most of my two trout, leaving only the lips that were still attached to the stringer. I was sitting in the shade and petting the dogs wondering if it was a muskrat or a mink, when one of the beagles burped, and I knew instantly what had happened to the trout. The bonus of this gluttony was that the beasts always followed me home obediently, hoping that I might drop a fish and they could eat it.

I knew that my summer was nearing the end when we went shopping for school clothes. Mom waited until August to purchase our school clothes, and then she bought our outfits just a wee bit big so they would make it until Christmas before we outgrew them. The first day of school always smelled like a department store, and the hallways squeaked with the sound that only brand new sneakers could make. An entire group of kids walking in a hall sounded like a basketball team running sprints. The new sneakers always quieted down after a couple weeks. I remember the first day of classes being a day of goodbyes and hellos. There were always kids that had flunked and were not returning to our grade, but we also usually gained a child or two that had managed to flunk into our class. This was back in the 1900s, when most students did not make the honor roll and failure was doled out by teachers in large servings. Many teachers could be seen weeping on the last day of school as they passed out report cards. I suppose it is possible that they were sad to see some kids go on to the next grade, but the most common cause for tears was their awareness that a certain child had flunked and would be returning the next year. Students would flunk for being lazy then. Laziness is now seen as a sign of artistic genius and a reason to reward the child with special exceptions and privileges in order to ensure that they pass. It was always viewed as a triumph if a bully flunked out of our grade, but all too often it was a friend that got held back to work on reading or math, and we would only get to see them after class and on weekends.

I was sad to see school start and be forced to spend so much time inside. I wanted to be with the dogs, chasing rabbits. I suppose that is why even as a kid I started doing my homework in the woods while listening to beagles chase. I had even devised a genius system of taking notes, because I found it too cumbersome to carry a notebook for each subject into the woods with me. I would carry the same notebook to all my classes until it was full. So let's say I started the day with history—I would take history notes. If I went from there to science class, I would just take science notes where I left off with the history notes. If I next went to math class, I simply turned the page and took math notes. The drawback was that when I studied for a biology test I would look at notes from Monday then I would have to page forward through the rest of the day before arriving at the biology notes for Tuesday. After reading those, I would page ahead to Wednesday's biology notes. So my notebooks were organized chronologically rather than by subject. When one book was full, I moved on to another. This sounds like a burden, but I could easily carry one notebook. I would run home and cut the dogs loose to run a rabbit while doing math drills or grammar assignments.

I could carry the notebook, a pencil, and even a textbook with some ease into the brush and get my homework done while listening to hound music. Pages were torn from the back of the notebook to turn in homework assignments. Pages were filled with notes from the front. Usually a notebook was filled hen half of the pages were consumed by homework assignments. As I remember things, we carried our books home in our hands. There is a school bus stop outside my office, and all of the kids look like Himalayan Sherpa, carrying massive backpacks that are more than capable of carrying every book they have been given. This begins in kindergarten, when they are carrying backpacks that they clearly will not grow into until fifth grade. I had one notebook most days.

It was nice to listen to the dogs while I did my homework, but I missed the fishing and staying outside all day long. Just the other day I ran dogs in this hot, summer sun, and they only lasted a half hour or so before showing signs of being hot. I put them in the dog box in the truck, gave them some water, and drove to Spring Creek on the way home. It is a famous trout stream in Pennsylvania, and all the guys on the river were from out of town and wearing Orvis clothes and driving luxury 4x4s. The river is catch and release only, but you don't have to use flies—it is just that almost everyone does. You can use other bait, if you want. I stood on the bank with a cheap fly rod and cast a few times with a red coachman. When the other anglers weren't looking, I removed the fly and turned over a few rocks until I found a crayfish. I put the tail meat on my hook and let it drift downstream. I instantly had a huge brown trout dragging the line. I fought him into the shore, looked at him, and then released the noble trout back into the water. I put a fly back on my fly rod and cast a few more times before finding another crayfish when the others were not watching me. Soon I caught another, much smaller trout. Everyone was trying to figure out what fly I was using. I carefully walked back to my truck—wearing brush pants, not waders—and returned home. Unlike my youth, I had a truck with an insulated dog box for my hounds to cool down, and I did not have to tie them to a tree in the shade. I released the trout rather than saving them for Jay. But I felt like a kid again, and the air certainly has that feel of school. Those guys are still trying to figure out what fly I had on my line. They probably never crawled on their bellies up to a stream bed with beagles running around.

CHRISTMAS COOKIES

The fact that I find fruit cake to be unappetizing is no secret. I am not entirely uncertain that one of the main ingredients is not stale candy corn that is still lying around, uneaten, from Halloween; if it is even possible for candy corn to go stale—it may be manufactured in a fashion that it is always stale, and therefore cannot go bad. My feelings are not the same, however, for Christmas cookies, perhaps because I have fond memories of those festive snacks.

My mother did not have a job when I was a kid. A job would have been too easy, and being issued a paycheck would have been too unexpected. Instead, she was a housemother, and therefore she just worked all the time, eliminating the negative feelings that we get when we "have to go to work." And since she wasn't paid, she never had to calculate her hourly wage, which is good, because she would have had a mathematical problem when dividing $0 by 168 hours for a week. Actually, it would have been fewer hours than that, because sometimes she would take a break from being a housewife and cut hair. Her specialty was old ladies who couldn't drive anymore, and she would go to their houses and "set" their hair. She would get paid on these outings, and much of it was used for fun stuff, after Dad's paycheck was spent on the bills. When I say fun stuff, I mean groceries; and maybe a movie once in a while. Of course it also helped a great deal at Christmas time.

She loved baking Christmas cookies. All sorts of them. There were wreaths made out of cornflakes and marshmallows, sugar cookies cut into various holiday shapes and frosted with every color, several styles that involved fudge, and a mega-cookie that started off as peanut butter cookie dough but had chocolate chips and several kinds of nuts added to them. Now, at that time there were only a handful of channels on television, which had nothing on them. Things are different now, as we can look through many channels before we realize that there is nothing on any of them. The home computer did not exist yet either, so you had to tell people what you did, rather than posting the intimate details of your life on Facebook.

Also, there was no caller I.D. This was a difficult era, when you had to answer the phone in order to tell who was calling. It therefore also follows that we had no cell phones, and you could not text your friends. So friends actually had to spend time together, and the side effect of such primitive days was that people developed manners and social skills. No doubt you can look up the definition of "manners" on the Internet now if you have forgotten what they are. I don't think they are discussed much now. They are as rare as an old carbureted engine today. All the people who can work on carburetors are in nursing homes, and it may well be that all the people with manners may be there before too many years as well.

Cookies were a big part of the December interactions that we experienced. People met in kitchens, rather than little restaurants and coffee shops, and all of the coffee had names that were pronounceable. A standard lunch while hunting would be a sandwich and cookies. The sugar cookies were the least desired, but they gave tired dogs a great burst of energy. I am sure they were way cheaper than those expensive energy bars that people give the hounds now. I remember the first energy bars for dogs had to be ripped in pieces and shoved into the beast's mouth with his mouth held closed until he ate it, much the same as when giving a pill to a dog. They must have tasted bad for a beagle to not eat them. Probably an old sugar cookie would work just fine, at least if the results I got feeding them to my pooches in my youth (and now) is any indication. Those of you pounding the field trial circuit will have to test the sugar cookie and let me know. They eat the sugar cookies voluntarily, too.

Some cookies kept me warm in the woods as well. It required great effort to chew them once they chilled to the same temperature as the outside air. So they were dunked in a cup of hot cocoa or coffee (depending on your age) to get them soft again. I remember placing gloves on the dashboard to be warmed and dried by the air that was defrosting the windshield of the truck that had sat all day during the hunt. We would put the cookies there, too—cornflakes held together by marshmallows makes for a jawbreaker at twenty-eight degrees. The hot air would thaw the marshmallow-glue until it was gooey and warm. They would make for a nice snack while driving home, after which we would return the hounds to the kennel and go inside for supper.

My wife is almost as passionate about Christmas cookies as my mother. There was a time when women guarded their cookie recipes in the same way that hunters refuse to reveal the whereabouts of a cherished hunting spot. Housemothers, however, are an endangered species, as most women have an employer. Housefathers appear to be on the rise, and it seems to be easy duty if you can get it. Most of the housefathers I know do not really clean or cook like housemothers, they just drive the kids to school and then pick them up at the end of the day, leaving the housework to the mother when she returns.

Anyway, moms can't find time to bake like they once did. My wife participates in cookie exchange programs, where you bake cookies, put them in a tin, and give them to another woman, accompanied with the recipes that produced the tin's goods. My wife receives cookies from other women, too. The goal, as near as I can tell, is to outdo your friends, both in terms of the complexity of the recipes and the decorative aspect of the tins that hold the cookies. I always know she is locked in culinary combat with another gal when she drives to Wegman's. Wegman's is a grocery store in our area that is designed, it would seem, for the antithesis of the housemother—the wealthy trophy wife who has a maid and enjoys spending three hours in a grocery store.

That being said, Wegman's has anything you would ever want. Stuff from all over the world. Many of the things you buy there are artisanal, meaning they are made by an artisan. I thought I knew what that word meant, but apparently, and I have discerned this from context, it really means overpriced. Artisanal bread costs enough to start up your own bakery. We never shop at Wegman's, but when the cookie competitions are going strong, she will bring back a bag of groceries (you know, those tiny plastic ones, not a big, brown, paper sack) from there and a receipt listing items that I never encountered. The kitchen then becomes a laboratory as she prepares to fill tins.

Herein lays the problem—my small pack of beagles live in the house. You always see people advertising coolers as being grizzly proof. They really ought to advertise them as beagle proof. There are few things as chaotic as when an athletic beagle is able to jump high enough so as to pull a container of cookies off the counter and onto the floor for all her pack mates to enjoy. Also, there are few things as embarrassing as meeting your buddies the next day for a rabbit hunt with fat, bloated beagles that gorged themselves on cookies the night before.

The safest place to store these items is on top of the refrigerator, as this is where the breakfast cereal must be stored from the dogs. I do not mean to give the impression that my hounds are not trained. In the field they handle better than most. They behave perfectly around food as long as they are being supervised. Beagles are often labeled as stupid, but I think obsessed is a better descriptor. They only have two thoughts—food and rabbits, and I am not sure that rabbits isn't simply the favorite food. The same stubbornness that lets them chase a rabbit until it is shot or hides in a hole also allows the merry beagle to have the patience of Job when it comes to waiting until it can be left alone in the kitchen without human supervision.

Now, we owned a child lock on the refrigerator. I say owned because it was broken by my mother-in-law, who could not figure it out. I can't complain about her not being able to solve adult things, as I often have to call my stepson to figure out the computer. The child lock was to prevent Lady, perhaps my most gluttonous beagle, from opening the refrigerator door. She swats it with her paw until it opens, and then she grabs whatever she can. If I am sitting in the kitchen, she behaves. It is only when you are in a separate room that we have this problem. We now block the refrigerator with the mobile dishwasher.

Cookies must emit a great deal of odor. Last Christmas we had the sugary treats on top of the refrigerator. One of the dogs must have pushed a kitchen chair close to the dishwasher. My hunch is that my oldest male is the culprit, as I have seen him move chairs by pushing them with his front paws while standing upright. This enabled Princess, Lady's daughter, to use the chair as a step to the surface of the dishwasher, which in turn was a launching pad to drag down the massive tub of cookies! I hunted the next day with four fat beagles. We now have a child gate to keep the dogs out of the kitchen entirely, all of which makes me wonder just who is training who in this relationship.

I am now judicious in taking cookies to the woods. In my youth I could eat as many as I wanted without gaining weight. I intentionally take the less desired sugar cookies now, so as to prevent myself from eating too many. Plus, there is no chocolate in them, which is poisonous to dogs. They still make a great snack for the pooches on a hunt, and I think they add a burst of energy to the hound work in the afternoon on an all-day hunt. The dogs are enthusiastic, and I keep from gaining weight by avoiding the tastier cookies. I can resist all the cookies that come through the house except for one batch.

The cookies I can't resist arrive as part of my wife's cookie exchange program. They all look familiar to me, so I know that the baker did not have to go to a specialty store to get the ingredients. Her cookies do not arrive in a fancy tin either; they are in a giant Cool Whip container, with each layer separated by paper towels. She is a retired housemother, or as close to retired as house moms get, which is to say she has grandchildren in her home much of the day as their parents work. Her recipes are written in a strange language that people no longer understand— pinches of this, a palm full of that, handfuls of other things. Dashes and splashes are common descriptors in the recipes. My wife ignores the recipe as if they were written in hieroglyphs. My mother has passed away, but these cookies, made by a grandmother, could pass as near replicas. I have been hunting a few spots that require a bit more hill walking, just so I can burn a few more calories as

I wait for this year's Cool Whip container to arrive. Merry Christmas, and I will see you at the kitchen table. We can lock the beagles outside in the yard.

PENNED UP

At the end of rabbit season I ran inside the club training pen for the first time in many months. The rabbits in there have many mowed paths to hop down, and they tend to start by running a circle that is actually the perimeter of the enclosure before embarking on a circuitous pattern that does not resemble a circle at all, but rather looks like a knotted kite string! What I like about the pen is the abundance of rabbits, especially in March, when my places to run in the wild seem to be depleted of bunnies. What I sometimes don't like about the pen is that same abundance of rabbits! A running pen with a high population density of bunnies can yield some screaming-hot chases, but the problem is that I know they are changing rabbits in the middle of the chase, and sometimes at an alarmingly high frequency.

It is as if the rabbits are running a relay race, and they simply run their leg of the chase before passing the job off to another bunny. They may even be passing a baton for all I know. I think I ruined a good pup once by starting it inside of a fenced area full of rabbits. The dog learned to simply run past a check and bump into a new rabbit and start running it. It sounded good to hear him chase! In hunting season, with rabbits far less abundant, I never knew if he was solving a three-minute check or jumping a new rabbit. He was at his best in that pen!

I like running pens, because there are professional rabbits in there. They do not hesitate to double back on their tracks and maybe even triple. They have had much experience. I sometimes mourn the loss of a good club rabbit. I once belonged to a club, and there was a big, stinky rabbit that hung out near the barn. Every morning I could find him there, and I think that I could recognize the look of him. I certainly felt that I could identify him by watching the chase. He always ran the same path for the first two circles. That rabbit performed like a champion for an entire summer. Then, one September morning, I could not locate him. I thought nothing of the matter, as it had happened before that he was not in his spot. After a few weeks I figured he either moved to another part of the enclosure or died. At any rate, those skilled rabbits provide good training and make my hounds look like a million bucks on a wild rabbit that has never seen a beagle!

I have known friends that hit the field trial circuit regularly who spend more time in the pen than I do. I let my beagles chase for a couple hours for my own enjoyment. The serious competitors need to be in better shape than that, and that is a fact. While I do not think that running inside enclosures causes dogs to handle poorly, I think it may sometimes give a beagler a little less incentive to work on teaching the dog to handle—the fence will keep Rover close at hand; and it is, after all, the chasing of rabbits that is key! This being the case, I have known a few trial dogs that are nearly impossible to handle outside a pen. Oh, you can still hunt with them, you just have to listen for the dog to start a chase and run over there as fast as you can. You are hunting with the dog, he isn't hunting with you.

Enclosures also provide a false sense of security. We have all had dogs get out of the pen on a rabbit. This is the reason why I rarely sit on the tailgate or nap in the clubhouse while the dogs are chasing. It doesn't take much of a hole for a rabbit to squeeze through it. I watched a full-grown rabbit run through my yard's chain-link fence so fast I thought I had a section missing. In reality, it squeezed through one diamond link without breaking stride. A small hole in a wire mesh rabbit fence at a club will let them get outside. A dog will soon follow. The rabbits know these holes and use them. A guy was recently running outside our club pen where he got a fantastic chase. The chase was then happening inside the fence. We were holding a trial, and no one was allowed to run inside the enclosure during that four-day period, except during the trial. The beagler, who was staying at the clubhouse for the weekend and was conditioning his dogs in the unfenced portion, said to the club president, "You have a hole in your fence."

"We checked it, we don't have any holes."

"I think my dogs are now in the pen," the guest beagler replied.

"Hey, I think you are right!"

The dogs were inside. The rabbit ran into the pen to try and get away, the opposite of what we normally experience. So I try not to allow a fence to give me a false sense of security. I presume there are always holes in the fence.

By far, my second favorite thing about a club pen is deer. I like having a place to readily identify a deer chase and break the dog from this nasty habit if it should happen. I would much rather do this at the club than in the wild on a deer chase that runs out of the county before I figure out that it is a trash run. In my home state it is legal to shoot and kill a dog that is attacking deer, and many people are overzealous to shoot a dog. I take this aspect of training very seriously. There is no shortage of people in the woods with guns that think my beagle can catch and kill a deer, and the same people think deer hunting is the only outdoor activity worthy of pursuit.

Years ago, when I was at Corning Beagle Club, we put up a six-foot, chain-link fence that was intended to prevent any dogs from getting out. And, as part of the fence was trenched, it did just that. It was high enough, however, for a deer to jump over of it, but a fawn could not. Well, fawns were born inside that fence and could not get out! Nothing breaks a dog better than a doe kicking the poor dog to protect her fawns! For a whole summer I worried about where that doe might be found with her fawns. She kicked the dog and broke him from ever chasing deer again, and she walked towards me a few times and forced me to move in another direction. Clubs are great for this training.

By far my favorite thing about a running pen is the fellowship. Members flock there to condition their hounds. You never know who you might see, or what dogs you might get to run against. Even though I do not field trial much, it is at these pens that I have seen my pot lickers run against field champions and do well on some days. It is at the running pen when I get to talk to other beaglers about things my wife and other friends just don't care to talk about. So despite the fact that there are a few aspects of enclosures that I do not like, I will be there for the summer getting my hounds ready for the months of October-February. We will be hunting then, and the hope is that the skills of the professional club rabbits make our season another success.

Aha!

Life has a way of producing moments when we
suddenly see things in perspective and accumulated data
in our minds rearranges itself and we understand
something more profoundly than we once did. Sometimes
we even say, "Aha!" I wish it happened more frequently for
me than it does. It happened to my wife, Renee, not so long
ago. She went on a health kick that involves her not eating
anything that contains milk or wheat. It wasn't due to an
allergy or anything, just something she saw from a doctor
who has a television show. Anyway, all sorts of things
started appearing in the fridge. Imitation cheese, various
gluten-free things, and milk made from almonds. I
understand that altering our diets is a necessary thing
sometimes.

My old hunting dog, Rebel, is on a special diet. It is a
dog food designed for canines experiencing kidney failure.
He has been eating it for a couple years, so it is at least
slowing his demise. Not long ago he had to have his
testicles removed to stop chronic prostate infections. It
broke my heart to check the "neutered" box when I
purchased his annual dog license, even if it did provide a
small discount in the fee that I paid to the county.

Anyway, he has been full of giddy up since the snip,
having more energy than he has displayed in a while.
When I leave the house I always make sure the beagles go
into crates, because they can't be trusted when we are not
home. Oh, they are house broke fine, but they will devote
their collective energy to stealing food from the refrigerator,
cupboards, shelves, and counters. The garbage isn't safe
either. Ever since the castration, Rebel has been hiding
behind the couch (or under the coffee table) to try avoiding
the crate when we are not home. He hopes I just forgot he
was not crated, or didn't notice. If I crouch low I can see
his eyes as he lays flat to the floor and remains motionless,

wedged between the sofa and the mopboard. I was trying to figure out what to use as a better snack (rather than moving the couch and grabbing him) when another change occurred in our refrigerator's contents—eggs. I am sure that they cost more money than they are worth, but my wife has started purchasing eggs that are already hard boiled and peeled, and stuffed into a re-sealable pouch that goes into the crisper drawer. She adds them to salads.

I suddenly remembered the veterinarian saying that egg was a good protein and that it was not bad for the kidneys. And to be honest, that old Rebel doesn't like the prescription food as much as what the other hounds get at chow time. He can smell the difference between his food and what they are eating. So one day last week, after all the other dogs went to the crate, I grabbed one of the eggs and waved it above the back of the couch, which was pushed up against the wall. I heard the tell-tale sounds of toenails on hardwood flooring and a tail alternating thumps between upholstery and the drywall. He walked out, head raised high, and nostrils flaring. Into his crate he went for a tasty treat. I started doing this every day before I left the house.

"Are you eating my eggs?" Renee asked.

"I've been using them a little bit," I answered. Notice my lie? I took credit for their absence, but neglected to tell her I was giving them to Rebel. That would be a waste of money in her eyes, (although maybe not, if I consider the cost of the prescription dog food he eats).

"Oh, okay," she answered.

If you are going to give a dog a dietary supplement of hard boiled eggs, I would suggest that you make the beast live outside. Dogs, of course, lack all basic manners regarding the gastrointestinal processes. They will belch or break wind in the room that you are occupying. I had to be married to my wife for years before she did either in front of me, and those were two isolated accidents. For the first two years of our marriage I only knew that she went to the bathroom because of the increased toilet paper usage in comparison to my single years. She, apparently, went into the restroom in silence, under the cover of darkness, and did her business. I would see a new roll of Charmin was on the roll, and that was the only evidence of her presence in that room other than showering. It was not unlike sitting in a deer stand from dawn till dusk without seeing a buck, only to find massive deer tracks in the snow upon returning the next day. Even then you can't prove it was a buck without proof, which is why trail cams are so common now. I wasn't going to put a trail cam in the bathroom ...

Anyway, beagles have no digestive manners like people. Not only will they fart in the same room, they will gladly do it on your lap. Their only manners are unintentional—they have a rather long, loud, and visually disturbing process when it comes to vomiting. This gives you time to scoop up the mutt in your arms and run towards the yard hoping you make it outside before detonation. There is no way to accurately estimate the length of a canine regurgitation fuse. Some burn slow, others are more accelerated. It's like firecrackers, so exercise caution by running with the dog facing in front of you and at arm's length in the event of a short fuse.

I digress. Rebel was napping on the floor next to the couch—not behind it, but in front of it. It was late at night after a long day. Renee was sprawled out on the couch, lying on her side with her head on the edge of the cushion. I'm not an interior decorator by any means, but I would estimate the distance between the floor and the top of the couch cushion to be somewhere in the neighborhood of "not very far." I was in the easy chair, watching Renee and Rebel sleep. Rebel was snoring, Renee was quiet, but her slowed breathing rate proved that she was asleep.

"PFFFFT," Rebel silently relieved the pressure on his belly. I can't say how long it took for the gas to rise the "not very far" distance, but it certainly hung there. It wafted in my direction as well. Soon I felt as if my chair were sitting in the middle of a paper mill town. Renee's slowed breathing stopped momentarily, and her eyes flashed open instantly. She sat bolt upright. Rebel awoke, too, thinking maybe she needed help with something, and jumped up to be with her. She had an aha moment, and if there was a thought balloon above her head like the comics have, it would have read, "I know where my eggs are going."

People panic when it comes to training beagle pups. They worry about how old a pup is when it will start chasing rabbits. They fret that the age when the baby beagle begins to bark on a scent trail will predetermine its overall ability. There is anxiety and worry from the very outset. We do tests with treats to try and determine the strength of the prospective puppy's nose. People get disappointed when a pup would rather play with a stick than smell a rabbit trail. We place them in talented packs of rabbit runners hoping that they figure it out by watching.

In my experience, a puppy begins chasing when the switch is flipped inside of his little noggin, and the age makes little difference. People think beagles are stupid, but they are simply not able to control their impulses, and their impulses exist primarily for food and bunnies. They are born with the food switch engaged. At some point between twelve weeks of age and maybe almost a year, a beagle's bunny switch flicks on. And it never goes off as long as they are alive. I teach just a few basic handling commands to my beagles for ease of control and safety. There is not much we can do to make them chase better. I know that when the moment happens they will sit up quickly with eyes wide open just like my wife did on that couch, and they will emit a bark that they have never made before—their rabbit song. It isn't the same as his bark for food, his bark while playing with kennel mates, or his bark at somebody coming near the house. It is his rabbit song, and he will sing it all his days. Renee sang a song that day she solved the mystery of the missing eggs, too, but it had a few bad words, so I can't tell you the lyrics.

Time

I'm not going to lie to you; there are days when technology aggravates me. My current truck is the only vehicle I have owned that has a simple clock to change whenever daylight savings time begins or ends. There is an "H" button for the hour and an "M" button for minutes. Whenever you press either one and hold it for a couple seconds it will begin moving slowly forward until you get the number you need. Then you just let go of the button. The truck that I previously owned required that the vehicle be started, the stereo turned on and set to AM, and the windshield wipers placed on the intermittent setting. Then the clock numbers could be changed by depressing a "clock" button and working the turn signals while pumping the brake. Well, that isn't exactly true—it was much more complicated than what I described, but I haven't owned the damn thing for a couple years, so I forget.

I was reminded of the way the world has changed not too long ago when my stepson left the house to meet a friend that had a car. When I was a youngster and a kid wanted to sneak out, the friend drove by the house and honked the horn. Anyone looking out the window would not see a vehicle and presume that the person was just saying hello. Such a thing is a long-past activity. Now the kid with the car parks close by and sends a text to your kid notifying him that he is outside waiting. Coincidentally, this is also the way that people say hello now—via text. I miss the days when people drove past the house and honked the horn. If I was outside, I simply lifted an arm to wave, often not looking up from whatever I was doing. A polite "horn hello" might happen with shocking regularity in a small town where everybody knew everybody else, especially if you lived where people had to drive past your house to go to town. If I was inside, I still sometimes lifted my arm in a wave, and that looked foolish if we were all sitting around the supper table. Hey, it was just a subconscious reaction.

My cell phone is often full of texts that say, "Hello, how are you doing?" Well, proper grammar would be too complicated, so they type "How R U" instead. Sometimes there are so many that I would not possibly have time to reply to everyone, so I just lift my arm in the air and make one long, prolonged wave. Sure, no one sees it, but to be fair I didn't see their texts either, because my cell phone normally sits inside the truck next to the clock that can be programmed so easily. Meanwhile, I have a perfectly functional telephone in my house that has a cord and everything. Nobody calls it.

As I was saying, daylight savings time is no problem in my current truck. It should be noted, however, that there are various digital clocks in my life that are a complete mystery to me. This problem is only compounded by the fact that my wife intentionally keeps some clocks reading a time that is a little ahead of the actual time. When I say it is a little fast, I mean somewhere in the vicinity of forty minutes. This, of course, would make no sense to a sane person. For my wife, however, it is how she makes sure that she gets to places on time.

"I trick myself into thinking it is later than it is, so that I am not late," she explained when we married.

"Hey, we are going to be late if you don't hurry up," I said one night, not long after we got hitched.

"Nah, that clock is forty-one minutes fast. We have time." She continued doing something with her hair. Naturally, we were late. The reason that the clock was forty-one minutes fast was because ten minutes wasn't nearly enough. So Renee periodically moves the clock a few minutes forward every time she thinks that she can do it and forgets that it was done. It isn't everybody that can trick themselves, but hey, deception is exactly what daylight savings time is all about. It isn't like we are really gaining time. It is just that we artificially put daylight on the backside of the day to make it seem like we have more of it.

The clock is irrelevant to both dogs and sportsmen. Dawn and dusk are sacred times of day, and no matter what the hands of the clock (or digital numbers) say, we instinctively know when those hours are approaching. As we approach St. Patrick's Day, I think of the Celtic notion of thin places or thin time. The ancient Irish Christians said that holy places were thin places—the boundary between this world and the next is thin there, and we can get glimpses of heaven. They also said the same thing about time—some times of the year are thin and blur the boundary between now and eternity.

Sunrise and sunset are like that for me. Even more specific, those few minutes of light before the sunrise (or after it sets) has a thinning effect on the boundary. It takes just over eight minutes for light to get here from the sun. So there is some light that oozes into our lives just before sunrise. It is as if the sun took aim and shot beams of daylight at us, and led us so that we would fly into it. The atmosphere scatters that light as well, so those precious minutes of light before sunrise are actually more than eight, and the same sky bends light so that we also get twilight after the sun sets as well.

Isn't that the time when fish bite, deer materialize out of the ground like they were raised to the surface on elevators, birds vocalize, and the underbrush comes alive with sound? It is a thin time indeed. Rabbits are crepuscular, a fancy word that says they are most active at twilight. It may help them stay safe from predators that dominate the night (owls, for one) or the day (hawks, amongst others). We often hear that rabbits can't be found in the afternoon, but the reality is that rabbits are present all the time, they just don't move as much in the middle of the day as they do when feeding at dusk and dawn. Eating rabbits are moving rabbits, and they leave scent trails for our hounds to find. A bunny that has been sitting in a form for hours has no fresh scent trails leading to his secluded spot. This is when the best jump dogs show their mettle by finding the rabbits in the forms.

The beagles and I are governed by the sun. We always know when the sun sets or rises. We try to get to the woods at one of those times each day for a chase. We fall asleep early at night, so we can be ready in the pre-morning. As the days lengthen we awaken a wee bit earlier each week.

Those hounds couldn't care less if we are on daylight savings time or not. Hunting season is only a few months, but they chase all year. Twilight is when they sing the songs of pursuit, and it becomes a heavenly sound for my ears at a thin time as I prepare my weekly sermons for the church I pastor. I always have a notepad, pen, and a Bible for saving ideas. It is all stowed safely in a one-gallon, zip-top bag in case of rain. As the light brightens, I may be walking, running after dogs, or sitting on a stump and reading scripture, but I am always thinking. The time of day and the mood music allow me to hear God a little bit better.

In recent months, my wife's self-delusion strategy of forwarding the clock has resulted in the alarm being exactly one hour fast. After daylight savings began, it then became two hours fast. Not long ago she still managed to be late, even though she had banked all that time. I was unaware of that dilemma, however, because the dogs and I were in the field appreciating the sacred time of dawn. But if you need to know what time it is in the Atlantic Ocean, she can tell you—that is the time zone her alarm clock is on.

CARDS

My wife has entered a strange phase in life where she makes her own cards. Now, if you price a greeting card at your local drug store, you will find that there isn't really much to the things, and I am guessing that there is a fairly high profit margin. Nine times out of ten the card you want to buy will not have the envelope you need, and that will result in your having to scour the card row, looking for one of the same size. I speak from limited experience, as I mostly buy cards on two occasions—my wife's birthday and our anniversary. Usually I buy them the day I need them, so I often get the first card that seems to be romantic enough to flip her emotional switch and get her to hug and mist.

Mist is a technical term I learned from officiating weddings. They always say, "A bride is beautiful when she mists." In other words, just a wee bit of tears. I always caution couples that misting looks beautiful, but the whole thing is a little less charming if the mist turns into a full-blown sob, the kind where the bottom lip is trembling but no sound is coming out of the mouth. The worst case of such a sob happened at a wedding I officiated in North Carolina, and it was the groom. The bride had a rather long procession down a lane that flanked a gorgeous lake during an outdoor ceremony. The groom's sob heightened in intensity, until it mutated into full-blown blubbering by the time we got to the vows. I am now an advocate of short processionals.

I was just glad that the bride asked me to be the clergyman for the ceremony. She is the baby sister to my childhood best friend, and she moved to the Carolinas as a little kid, her brother was a senior in high school at the time. Her only memory of me as a youngster was walking into her family garage (a huge garage at that) whilst her brother and I were playing floor hockey in the winter, practicing shots at a goal that was smaller than we would be shooting at in a game. I sent a slap shot ricocheting off her cheek, in a scene not altogether dissimilar to the Brady Bunch episode where Marsha got wacked in the nose by a football—if Marsha was a pre-school kid and the football was a hard, half-frozen plastic ball moving at a scorching fast velocity. The poor kid got in trouble with her mom, too, because she was repeatedly told not to go out in the garage while we were playing hockey.

Anyway, purchasing cards is not something I have done very often. So when my wife decided to start making her own cards, I figured it was to save money. Well, that is like saying we rabbit hunt to save money on meat. I have a formula that says the cost per pound is (HG + BE)/lb., wherein HG is hunting gear (annual expense of guns, ammo, clothes, gasoline, etc), HE is hound expense (health care, food, treats, etc), and lb. is the total pounds of meat from the rabbits on any given year. Standard values of rabbit meat by this formula run about $976.56 per pound, if you love new shotguns, miss a lot of bunnies, drive a truck, and spoil your dogs.

I hate to tell you what the cost might be for a handmade card. Certainly you could not afford to buy one of these things if you paid the card manufacturer the minimum wage. Heck, they are too expensive if the card maker was being paid the same wages as a waitress, or even a migrant fruit picker. Granted, I do not pay too much attention to the card making process, but I think my father could churn out a new kitchen with handcrafted cabinets faster than my wife can produce one birthday card. So a few weeks per card would be my estimation.

Card making, I believe, fulfills a similar role to quilting for other women. I once served a church, and the women's group would quilt every week. They worked on their own projects, but they always made a baby quilt that they donated to an organization that provided baby quilts for infants that died, many of which were born with AIDS. It was a sad ministry, but the women enjoyed each other's company and had fellowship time. There were snacks, and sometimes they went to eat lunch afterwards. My wife, and many other people of her generation, cannot use a needle.

We do not own thread, as far as I can tell. I sew missing buttons back on with fishing leader. I presume it is waterproof. So in an impersonal world with form letters and e-mail blasts, they make very personal cards.

Here is where I get involved. She wants to incorporate a picture of the beagles into the Christmas cards that she makes for everyone this year. Now, my first thought is this: I hope she started in January if she plans on making enough cards, and that she hasn't been distracted by other miscellaneous cards for anniversaries, birthdays, graduations, hospitalizations, or deaths. Her card making supplies are in a small room of the house, but it contains as much inventory as an entire craft store. To be fair, there is also scrap booking supplies in there. Trust me when I tell you that there are no scraps in a scrap book. They sell the paper for scrapbooks by the sheet, and you could buy veneer wood from a cherry tree for less. At any rate, her card/scrap booking room is much like Oscar the Grouch's garbage can from Sesame Street, in the sense that it certainly holds a much greater volume than the measurements of the external dimensions of the space would indicate as possible. Some sort of quantum physics is at play, no doubt, and I am not sure that an event horizon from a black hole does not exist at the threshold of "Renee's room," as we call it. I have gone in there several times, but I wandered for hours in the maze and feared I may not get out. At one point I thought I saw a Minotaur. I borrowed a pair of scissors one time, only to be surprised by the fact that it did not cut a straight line, but rather it created decorative borders and designs to be attached to a card. Periodically we hear a muffled slump from the room as entropy exerts itself, and a pile of this and a stack of that merge. It is these accumulated slumps that I think have produced sufficient gravity to form the black hole.

My second worry, besides her not having enough time to make these cards (and it is only November as I write this) is that I have no idea how to get beagles to pose for the picture she wants. You know how people always have their dogs standing tall and still on the cover of the magazine? I have never taught a dog to do that. I have never owned a field champion, so there has never been a need to get a perfect stud position for a portrait. Ever been to a U.B.G.F. trial and seen that hound sitting and turning and trying to jump off the bench as the show judge looks it over? That would be mine, standing all slouchy and trying to get back in the brush or putting its front paws on the judge's chest looking for a scratch behind the ear.

I did show Renee some pictures of my dogs after the hunt, sitting all tired and sniffing dead rabbits.

"Really?" she asked. "Those are pictures you think we can use?"

"Why not, they are calm?"

"Because," she moved her arms from being crossed on her chest to holding her hands on her hips in order to emphasize my stupidity, "you can't say Merry Christmas! Here are dogs smelling the hind ends of dead animals!" She then waved her arms outward before returning them to a crossed position.

"What about these?" I showed her pictures of the dogs chasing rabbits.

"Is there a dog in this picture?" she squinted. "All I see is a blur."

"Yeah," I grinned. "It is hard to get a good picture of a running beagle, and I thought the blurriness would be a nice touch—it shows how fast they are chasing!"

"What is wrong with you?" Her hands returned to the hips. "THINK CHRISTMAS!"

"Then we will have to get pictures of them sleeping after a chase. I may have a few," I said. She returned to the black hole, and I went to see about making more photos of dogs smelling hind ends. After all, if they got good and tired while hunting, they might later snuggle together in a tri-color pile on the couch in the evening and present the cute sort of pose that she is looking for.

Maybe I will include a year-end letter to put in her card, too. The additional weight will be miniscule. There is no way that these cards are shipping on one stamp. Just the weight of glue alone is substantial, as these cards are layered like the feathers on a bird with multiple laminated layers of colored paper. When viewed in profile, they look like half inch plywood. There must be several pounds of glitter, too. Additional weight is packed on from the ink with cute stamps. Industrial-strength envelopes are handcrafted from stout cardboard and paper grocery sacks. I am not sure, but we might be better off mailing them in one of those priority envelopes that are the same cost no matter the weight. When she drops a finished card on the table, it lands with a thud like a phonebook. It would probably be cheaper to mail a pound of rabbit meat to everyone, shipped with dry ice.

But if I write one of those letters, I want to write a real one. Most people paint some rosy picture of the previous calendar year, emphasizing all the achievements of the family members before wishing the reader a Merry Christmas. No one mentions the negative stuff that can characterize at least parts of the year. I would tell you the juicy stuff. About getting lost in the woods, and getting a flat way out in the middle of an old coal stripping. I would tell you about leaving the house with my shirt inside out, although kids seem to do that on purpose now. You would read about the dogs and a few encounters with critters such as skunks. I might tell you about the death of the chipmunks as the beagles cornered them under the shed in the yard when it was too hot to let them chase rabbits and how bad chipmunk breath really smells on a hunting dog. The letter might detail the night last spring when we went to dinner and returned to find our house looking like a bunch of college kids had a party, as the beagles got the refrigerator open in our absence and rifled through the shelves and drawers, leaving packaging and wrappers strewn everywhere. The mutts all were laying in a coma-like misery, bloated with food, and moaning like college kids with a hangover. Maybe I will narrate the story of this amazing bunny that ran for several hours and never gave me a shot, and when I saw it I was too thankful for the hound music to shoot it. Surely I will tell you about the misery of having house beagles when a female is in season and the males bark themselves mute.

Well, I guess such a letter would not be permitted in this card, it just wouldn't fit in with the goal we have in mind. I mean the picture we want to paint in this card is of sleeping, calm beagles, not AKC registered gluttons that only think about rabbits and food. A snapshot, even if fictitious, is what we want at Christmas. Reality is too much to take. No one wants to look at Christmas as the story of a poor, single mother who gave birth to a kid in a barn, noticed only by foreigners and the people who were outside in a field. But that is what we are celebrating, an outcast who came to save all outcasts. Merry Christmas.

LUNCH

My mother was great at packing a lunch. She did it every day for my father, and she also made my lunch on many days. When I went to school, back in the 1900s as my stepson, Wesley, says the school cafeteria was a much more basic institution than it is now. First of all, there was no breakfast being served before classes then. It was strictly lunch. Also, choices were much more limited. Wes goes to school and gets a choice of three or four meal options. We had two choices—whatever they decided to cook that day or peanut butter sandwiches. The peanut butter sat in a large mixing bowl on a table next to where you paid for your lunch. The bowl was cold and the peanut putter was more like peanut brittle, so my hunch is that they just stashed the massive mixing bowl in a cooler at the end of each day and added peanut butter to said bowl whenever it got low.

Peanuts, because of allergies, are now viewed with the same suspicion as asbestos and mercury, and so it is not found anywhere near a cafeteria. There was a time when kids were expected to know their allergies and judiciously refuse to eat anything that might cause troubles. Now the schools are expected to monitor these things. So forget peanut butter or strawberries, they are gone along with any other foodstuff that tends to rank amongst the more common allergies. Anyway, my mother read the weekly lunch schedule in the newspaper and had a real good idea about what I would not like, so she packed my lunch on those days. Milk money was the only money I would need on those days.

Oh, kids today do not have to handle lunch money. There is no need to deal with a bully that might take it, and no need to worry about losing it. Parents send money in advance to an account, and their kids can eat as much as they want. When the account gets low, an e-mail is automatically sent to the parents so that the kid's lunch fund can be replenished. We also get e-mails that alert us to Wesley's academic progress. Reading these emails side by side, I would say that his best class is definitely lunch. It costs more to feed him lunch for a day than I eat at lunch for a week. I learned all of this the hard way while his mother was out of town for work.

"Okay." I looked at him as I retrieved my billfold from my back pocket on my first morning watching him alone. "How much is lunch? It was sixty cents when I was in elementary school."

He blinked at me.

"Do you know how to count money?" I said to the kid.

"I don't know how much it is." He was looking at a game screen in his hand.

"Here," I said. "Take ten bucks, bring back the change. I will then know what it costs."

He returned with no money. He didn't know where it went either. His mother called that night. "Hi, honey," I said. "How is your conference?"

"I wanna talk to my baby boy! Put Wes on the phone!"

"Oh. Umm, sure. Hey, how much does a school lunch cos—"

"PUT MY KID ON THE PHONE!"

"Your mama wants to talk to you," I said. "I want to ask her something when you are done."

He blinked at me like he did that morning. He chatted a bit and then hung up.

"Hey, did you tell her I wanted to ask her something?" I said as the kid handed me the phone.

"No, I forgot." He blinked at me and returned to a hand-held screen.

"Okay," I spoke slowly to him the next day, the way you might to a visitor from another nation who could read English but had little experience in real conversations. "Here is ten more dollars." I put the money in an envelope and duct taped it to the inside of his backpack.

"Put your change in the envelope and bring it home," I annunciated loudly, as if he might be a nearly deaf visitor to our nation. Again, he returned with no money.

I called his mother. "Is it an emergency?" she sighed. "I'm in a meeting."

"I think I am out twenty bucks," I groaned.

"I don't have time for th—" she began to hang up on me.

"So, I ain't sure Wes is eating at school," I said, appealing to her maternal instinct.

"Hold on," she whispered, and I heard the distinct sounds of her shoes walking quickly on a linoleum or tile floor and then the sound of a door. "Is my baby boy okay?!" she screamed.

"Sure," I said. "If you consider staring at a hand-held video game okay, which I presume you do."

"Is he hungry?"

"He doesn't seem it," I said and then explained the missing twenty bucks.

"Are you nuts?" she said to me. "Kids have an account at the school. They don't pay every day."

I then launched into a fine soliloquy about kids needing to learn responsibility and how to count money and knowing the value of a dollar. The reason it was a soliloquy was because my wife had hung up on me. At least in the 1900s you heard the "click" that let you know your conversation partner had hung up the phone. In the age of cell phones you just sort of ramble for a little bit until you realize that you are talking to nobody.

Anyway, my mother was a master of packing a lunch on some days and giving us cash on others. She gave us each a freshly ironed one dollar bill after the cost of lunch jumped to seventy-five cents. The quarter in change could be used for an ice cream, which the school sold during the last few minutes of lunch, generating a near riot on days when the menu was less appetizing (tuna casserole, or any of the assorted "loaves" or patties"). She had the habit of ironing all of our clothes the morning that we wore them— including socks and underwear—and she simply took the wrinkles out of a couple dollar bills before giving them to us so that they looked presentable when we paid for our food, rather than like they were hauled out of my father's front pocket.

"Your money is always so crisp and wrinkle-free," the lady who took the money said to me when I was in seventh grade.

"You should see my underwear," I said. Looking back on that conversation as an adult, I can see why she gave me a bewildered look. It would not be easy to make the mental leap that my mother ironed both underwear and money—two things I thought were not worthy of an iron.

One of the best parts of any hunting day was when we would go to the tailgate, give the dogs some water, and eat our lunch while we talked about the morning hunt and planned the afternoon. Thermoses of coffee, cocoa, and soup were common sights. Sandwiches were made on thick cuts of homemade bread so that they did not get soggy, and they were wrapped in wax paper. There was always a bit of dessert in recently emptied and cleaned, plastic butter containers. There were even a few dog biscuits shoved into a plastic bag to give the beagles.

"Nice shooting!" was something said while eating lunch on a tailgate. The chases got longer, the shots further, and the breakdowns in the chases fewer while eating at the truck. Sometimes there were pickled eggs and beets. I worked one summer during high school for the Allegheny National Forest, which allowed me to find great spots for chasing snowshoe hare. Our lunches sat in a locked van (forestry green in color) all morning as the sun beat through the windows. A ham sandwich would wither in that environment, and the mustard just became overpowering. She froze my sandwich the night before as a solution, so that it was thawed but cold at lunch time. It was perfect for a hot, summer day.

Eating lunch in a restaurant, while rabbit hunting, doesn't have the same appeal to me. I feel self-conscious wearing muddy boots into even the most informal places. It also looks funny if you run out and give a bit of crust to your dog and then return to your table. Poking a bit of bread into the dog crate, however, seems perfectly normal. Plus, being in a building puts you on other people's time schedules—the cooks, the wait-staff, and the other customers eating lunch. I like to eat and get back to the briars.

BOB FORD

Even now, as I think of those great fall hunts, I do not know when Mom made those lunches. Was it after I went to bed? Before I awoke? She always baked cookies or pie the night before a hunt so we had some the next day as well. She cooked rabbit on Sundays, even though it wasn't her favorite. Her cocoa was made with milk, not water. These are the sorts of things that seemed ordinary when she was alive, but special since she has died. I think I will invoke a rule with my hunting partners this year that mandates tailgate lunches and no restaurants. Happy Mother's Day.

THANKSGIVING HUNT

At any large family gathering there can be a problem
with seating. Thanksgiving is just such an occasion. In
these circumstances there is always a kids' table—
frequently a flimsy or collapsible table. This is often viewed
as a less honorable seat than others. I, for one, always
volunteer to sit at the kids' table. The conversations are
much better. The adult table mostly talks about work,
social status, or some other form of gossip. They can
obsess over matters of relationships. "You do too know
Anna. She was married to that Smith kid who was a cousin
to the fellow who got his truck stuck last winter, and it sat
there till spring. Know who I mean?" Of course you don't
have any idea who they are talking about and you also
have no idea where this conversation might be headed. It is
also a table fond of talking about who died, who is dying,
or who should be dead by now. Adults love to make
instantaneous decisions about someone, based solely upon
their paternity. It also seems to matter a great deal where
someone works and what they do there.

"I haven't seen your cousin Tim in forever. Where is he
working now?"

"He is working as a janitor at a big company."

"Oh, I see," says a judgmental voice. "Well, you know,
some people don't have a job at all ..." Only adults can be
so lame as to think that a person's occupation means all
that much as to determining the worth of a person. The
seminary I attended had a gruff supervisor of the
maintenance department. I worked in that department,
and we all did double duty as janitors and repairmen. Our
supervisor, Gene Vest, had no college classes under his
belt—he was hired for his expertise in repairing things. The
seminary had a chaplain who was supposed to be the main
counselor and caregiver to the souls of the students. I
forget what her name was, to be honest, because in many

ways it was Gene that provided spiritual direction for much of the campus, not just the crew under his direction, but everyone. Professors would frequently drop in to chit chat about their woes, and there was no shortage of coffee as Gene filled people's cups to ease their pain. My alma mater is in Ohio, but lots of Pennsylvania Methodists went there. Gene always said he had a special place in his heart for his PA employees, because we were the ones who always fulfilled our work study in his department. I always ran out of work study hours in the first month, and Gene put me on payroll, paying for my wages with his departmental budget, allowing me to work as many hours as I wanted. To some of the more arrogant faculty he was "in charge of the janitors." His funeral was standing room only, as faculty and staff drove from just north of Columbus to Gene's hometown in the Ohio River Valley for the service. I can still hear Gene whistling hymns. Don't tell my worship professor, but when we were given an assignment to write the words to our own hymn, I was lost. So Gene did it for me, patting me on the back and filling my coffee cup.

Anyway, I digress. The kids table, by contrast, has much more interesting conversation. Like conversations about superheroes. Or ten-speed bikes versus BMX. What school meals are so bad that a lunch must be packed, and what should be packed in that lunch. Not all sandwiches are equal. How to tell when to ask mom or dad for money was a good conversation I once had at the kids' table. Their answer was quite brilliant—always ask Dad after he plays golf, always ask Mom after she watches *Jeopardy* and guesses all the answers right. You see what I mean? Much better conversation.

One Thanksgiving my sister's oldest kid said, "Do you know what tomorrow is?"

"No, kiddo, what is it?" I said.

"It is Good Friday!" She was very excited.

"No, that is in the spring," I said. "The Friday before Easter."

"No, silly!" she grinned. "It is tomorrow when we go shopping for Christmas!"

"Oh," I said. "You mean Black Friday."

"It is a good day!"

"Well," I started. "It is called Black Friday because it is when the stores get out of the red and into the black by making money." Right away I could tell that I had accidentally injected nonsensical adult conversation into the kids' table. "Forget that, what are you shopping for?"

"I wanna get my mom a new set of cookie cutters for Christmas cookies. She loves making cookies." And the kid was right, my sister does love baking cookies, and she does get excited about the shapes of Christmas cookies. Over at the grown-up table I could hear a discussion on politics, and was glad that I was not sitting there. The kids' table had moved on to an in-depth analysis of the virtues of fruit pie versus pumpkin pie with Cool Whip.

So I think that perhaps this may be part of the key to living a good life—always maintaining the rigorous standards of the kids' table even after we become adults. Granted, there are occasional problems at the kids' table, a few misunderstandings, a little bit of hurt feelings, maybe even an outburst; but it is all done with integrity. There are no back-handed compliments, no veiled insults, and no false modesty.

"You do pretty well, all things considered," is not said there. They would say, "Wow! Good job!"

"No, no, don't make a big deal about my birthday," is likewise never uttered when the real intent of such a statement is, "Hey, my birthday is coming up, let's do something fun!" In the end, life is too short to be become an adult, at least not as I have described such maturity here. I suppose that is why my wife constantly reminds me that I am being immature.

"Why can't you ever where a tie to a formal occasion?" she said to me on our way to the open house at the school our kid attends. She thought the lack of a tie was immature until I asked his teacher, "So is this permanent record teacher's talk a scare tactic or a myth?" That really got me labeled as immature, but I can honestly think of no instance, whatsoever, where my permanent school record was ever consulted. At no point did any employer ever say, "Mr. Ford, you can't work here. While the background check has shown that you have never been arrested, we did turn up some disturbing information on your high

school's permanent record. It seems that you once got
suspended from school for intentionally eating raw leaks
and making your breathe stink. All to avoid a French test.
FOR SHAME!"

There are so many ways that I have refused to grow up.
I still have trouble sleeping the night before hunting season
opens. A beautiful autumn day always places thoughts of
hooky in my mind. I still get just a little depressed if I go
rabbit hunting and don't get any, though I won't admit it. I
pour over hunting and fishing catalogs at night, dreaming
of exotic hunts, when I should be trying to get sleepy. No
fancy omelet can ever be as good of a start to a hunt as
Golden Grahams. During an all-day rabbit hunt, I love to
sneak a little people food to the dogs when no one is
looking. If I am a little scared, I insist on having a dog sleep
at the foot of my bed. If I can shoot my daily limit without
dirtying both barrels of my shotgun, I get more than just a
little pleased. Sad news always makes me take the dogs for
a rabbit chase. I buy special snacks for my dogs on their
birthdays and make sure they get to go chase a rabbit that
day, even if I have to rearrange my whole schedule. I
always dissipate anxiety and nervousness by twirling a
beagle's ear with my hand. I like to sharpen my pocket
knife, and I am secretly pleased to let someone use it when
a blade is required. Hearing a puppy bark on a rabbit for
the very first time is my favorite sound. If you see me
staring out into space and daydreaming, I may well be
thinking about living off the land as a professional
houndsman. My brush pants are still the most expensive
pair of pants I own. Sometimes, if hunting or a field trial is
going well, I get too excited to eat lunch. I still like having a
campfire in the yard after a successful hunt in the early
fall, and the best part is falling asleep on a bench beside
the fire with the beagles snug against me, shielding me
from the night air. It is essential to cook an extra hot dog
for the beagles to share; even if that means that I don't get
to eat one. I prefer to have my hounds go to the bathroom
in the woods and have no comprehension of people walking
their dog on the street with a poop bag on their hand.
School cancellations due to large snowstorms make me as
excited as they did when they had the potential to cancel

my own classes. I pity beagles that live on a chain for the entirety of the year, except the first month of rabbit season. The sound of a pack of beagles on a sight chase makes me feel more alive. Oh, and lest I forget, I always go rabbit hunting on Thanksgiving.

And that is the beauty of Thanksgiving—being a kid. Kids don't worry about invited guests for the feast or when the meal will be eaten, since there are plenty of snacks to graze upon until the table is set. The logistical problems caused by several women competing to cook in one kitchen means nothing to a kid. No child begins the long Thanksgiving break from classes with plans of worrying about school work every day until he returns. I am not sure why adults perpetually worry about work until they get back. Youngsters will spontaneously break into a game of football in the yard while the bird cooks, where adults need to confirm any sort of recreation days (or weeks) in advance. Kids will get out of bed early on a vacation day so as to extract the maximum amount of fun, while an adult's preference is to sleep in until after the clock indicates the start of a typical workday. It seems obvious that immaturity has a vital role in life.

So I will hunt all morning on Thanksgiving, and not worry one bit about a need to entertain any in-laws or relatives. I will pack pie and dried sweet corn for my lunch and wash it down with a thermos of coffee. We never eat the big meal too early, so I will stop at a place close to home after lunch. It is not a large tract of land, but it always yields one great chase. Oh, and I might bring some of those expensive pig ears from the store for the dogs to eat on the way home. This should get me home around two. It is then the perfect time to visit with relatives and eat. After everyone leaves I will have a campfire in the yard and cook hotdogs for the hounds before we doze. Well, actually, I will have a little fire in the wood pellet stove located in the living room and nuke the frankfurters in the microwave. Then the dogs and I can nap properly on the couch—that cold, hard bench makes me ache. Cripes, even if I am immature, I am over forty, you know! Happy Thanksgiving.

WINNER'S PACK

"What time are we going to run dogs tomorrow?" I asked Andy last summer at his place of work.

"How about six o'clock tomorrow morning," he scratched his beard.

"Sounds good to me!" I exclaimed. Knowing Andy, I was certain that I would have an hour to see what my dogs could do before he dropped a few field champions (or future field champions) from his DeadRiver kennel to chase the rabbit with my regular old hunting dogs. Sure enough, he pulled into the running grounds at a quarter after seven, and by then I had coffee made from the clubhouse pot.

"Want some coffee?" I offered.

"I have some," he held a mug up, "that's why I am late."

"It took you an hour and a half to make coffee?"

"Relax. I am not an hour and a half late. I am only an hour and fifteen minutes late." He dropped the tailgate and put some professionals on the ground to show my knucklehead hounds how to run a rabbit. And then we got to the tailgate.

There are various ways to evaluate a chase. Some guys can keep up with the hounds and follow them. Those are the sprinters. Some guys can get in front of the chase, watch the rabbit and beagles go past, and then run again to intercept the chase a little further along. Then there is tailgating. That is Andy's way. Tailgating is a great way to begin a morning of conditioning hounds. You sit on the tailgate and listen to the run. Coffee is a big part of this. In the summer when the gnats run kamikaze missions at your eyes and the mosquitoes feast on your skin, it can be miserable, until Andy would get his tobacco and pipe and sit back on the tailgate, and puff away like Gandalf in the Lord of the Rings movies. The bugs beat a hasty retreat.

"That sounded like your Hoss getting that check," he said.

"That wasn't my dog."

"Are you sure?" he interrogated me. "That wasn't one of my dogs. Trust me, that was Hoss." Of course it wasn't my dog. It was one of Andy's. But that is the way it goes—Andy compliments your hounds, and he never brags about his success at trials. Actually, he says all the success belongs to the dogs, not him.

"Anyway," I sipped my coffee, "we can't tell anything by sitting on this tailgate."

"We can listen to the music," Andy corrected me.

That was true. We could hear the music. Oh, we had a good idea what the dogs were doing because we had run together so often. We knew which dogs liked to take the front and run a little mute to get a head start. We knew which dogs would take a big "walkabout" romp on a tough check hoping to stumble on the rabbit's trail. We knew which dogs were most prone to solving a double. No, you can't evaluate a pack from the tailgate, but you can make very educated guesses about what is happening if it is a pack that has run together frequently. That's the case for Andy and me.

We meet in the early hours before he has to be at work at Lion Country Supply when the mornings are still cool, but I think Andy prefers the heat of late summer. He likes to run at night. There is always a part of summer when midnight is no cooler than dawn. We ran one night a couple summers ago and had to pull porcupine quills from a few hounds before we went home. Something about rabbit feeders and brush piles seems to attract porcupines into a beagle club in larger numbers than in the wild.

"This stinks!" I yelled as we struggled to hold a dog still and get a quill out.

"That ain't the worst stink," he said.

"What?"

"I smell skunk, and it is on your house dog over there about 50 yards," he muttered through teeth that were clenching his pipe as he puffed away a swarm of sweat-seeking insects.

"I despise night running." I went to my trunk for the "mostly" effective anti-skunk spray from my truck.

"I love it," he drug out the word love in a slow, gravelly sort of way, "it's easier to stay up late than it is to get up early!"

All through the grueling field trial season, he would be up late and conditioning hounds. When the mercury soars a great dog has to be in great shape. Andy insists on conditioning. We were out late one night last summer listening to the hounds, and I said, "I'd like to look for a derby to run next year." There was no reply.

The next day I got a text message. It said, "I have a derby for you."

I called him, and the ringer was squelched to voicemail.

"I'm at work and can't talk," he texted.

If you have never been to Lion Country Supply, which advertises in all the beagle magazines, it is a small store in the front, and a massive warehouse in the back. There are a few desks back there where the employees are answering the phones. Andy's desk has some plaques that narrate some of the greater achievements his hounds have accomplished. They were issued from major trials or consistency awards. They aren't on display in his house for all visitors to behold—probably there as a bit of good news on days when the phones are ringing off the hook. If you ever had a GPS question and called the store, you probably talked to Andy. He is the GPS guru. He would be on the phone and helping guys as a person who not only sells equipment, but has tested it all. He knew the pros and cons. His boss gave him the new Garmin Alpha before it was on the market and said, "See how good it is so we can serve our customers." Anyway, back to the text conversation ...

"I have a dog that I think will be a good derby. He runs a good rabbit."

"Okay," I texted back.

"Come get him. He is in my truck."

"What?"

"Run him. See if you like him. His name is Badger."

I ran the dog, and I liked him. He told me to keep the dog for as long as I wanted to evaluate the beagle. Who does that? I ran him for a month, and when we were out running dogs one night I said, "How much do you want for Badger?"

"He ain't for sale," he muttered while biting his pipe.

"What?"

"Well, I would sell him to you. But if you don't want him, I am not going to sell him to anyone else."

"I gotta pay ya!" I insisted.

"Whatever you think is fair," he patted me on the back, assuring me that money wasn't what was happening here.

I texted him at work one day and asked if he was able to fix my GPS if I stopped. I told him I was just leaving the Altoona Hospital from doing hospital visits. He can't talk on the phone at work, remember? Ten minutes later my phone rang.

"Hello?"

"How close are you to the store?" Andy sounded urgent.

"Not far."

"Can you stop at the Subway in Bald Eagle?" he asked. "I forgot my lunch at home."

"Sure," I said. "What do you want?"

"Oh, I will text it to you. It's a pretty involved sandwich."

It was an elaborate order, including a very specific brand of chips that had to be the proper style (Barbeque maybe) and size. I entered the store with food and GPS. He ran to the back, fixed my collar, and upon returning he insisted on paying me for the food. Things like that have happened a lot. I would stop at the store, and Andy would come out, and we would talk rabbit dogs, make hunting plans, discuss new spots, and laugh. Always lots of laughing. I have a job that can be less than fun. I go to hospitals and nursing homes and funeral parlors. Beagles are a pleasant distraction from all of that—I have never been the biggest competitor on the field trial circuit—I can't even attend a Sunday trial without taking vacation! Andy has always been my welcome friend to forget all the negativity. You can't find him in a bad mood. He is never argumentative (rare in beagling!) and he is mellow. Real mellow—keeps things in perspective. There are guys that despise each other, and they both love Andy. I officiated

Andy's wedding when he and his wife Lisa married. It was an outdoor ceremony, on 12-12-12 on top of a hill in a wind gale. After dark. The orders were to wear hunting clothes.

I drove Andy to the top of the hill, and on the way up I said, "How the hell am I gonna read the liturgy up there. It's dark."

He pulled a coon hunting light from his pocket and strapped it to his forehead, "How is this?"

"Yeah, man," I said, "just look at this book through the ceremony so I have light."

In a lot of ways he shined a light of happiness everywhere. I always appreciated that light. He certainly lifted my spirits whenever I left a nursing home where a woman was distraught as her Alzheimer-ridden husband did not recognize her, or after a hospital visit with a patient diagnosed with terminal cancer. One winter I had two funerals in eight days, both were babies. Andy and I went hunting. And as I write this, I am preparing to preside at Andy's funeral. Gone too soon from this world. He never bragged about his dogs, but his DeadRiver kennel finished five field champions in a short time—Dixie, Rebel, Ruby, Ranger, and Bell, all within a little less than a decade. But it is not his competitive spirit that I will miss, but his compassionate side. His joy and his laugh are emblazoned upon my mind. He died peacefully in his sleep eagerly anticipating a rabbit hunt the next morning, where he was going to introduce a friend's kids to the exciting world of hunting with beagles. When I got the news, I held my own DeadRiver dog real close. I use different analogies for heaven at different funerals. This week the analogy will be winners' pack. He certainly was a winner who would do anything for anybody.

Andy Purnell February 10, 1966-January 3, 2015

Made in the USA
Middletown, DE
28 June 2015